Israelis, Jews,
and Jesus

Israelis, Jews, and Jesus

PINCHAS LAPIDE

Translated by Peter Heinegg

Foreword by Samuel Sandmel

DOUBLEDAY & COMPANY, INC., GARDEN CITY, N.Y., 1979

This book was originally published in German under the title *Ist das nicht Josephs Sohn?: Jesus im heutigen Judentum* (© 1976 by Calwer Verlag, Stuttgart, and Kösel-Verlag GmbH & Co., Munich).

ISBN: 0-385-13433-9
Library of Congress Catalog Card Number: 77-82767
Translation and Foreword Copyright © 1979 by Doubleday & Company, Inc.

Foreword

About a generation ago Conrad Moehlman of Colgate-Rochester Seminary wrote a book, *The Christian-Jewish Tragedy*. Central to that tragedy have been two enigmas. The first of these is the paradox that the man Jesus was a Jew but Christianity became rather quickly a completely Gentile movement.

It has not been too difficult for scholars to show how the young movement, on crossing the borders from Judea into the Greek world, became Hellenized. It has not been too difficult to show that the words of the common Jewish-Christian book vocabulary, such as messiah, sin, and righteousness, came to have meanings and values different in Christianity from those they have in Judaism. It is not too difficult to point out that Christianity was a very actively missionary religion and Judaism so only passively. Yet these developments in no way contribute substantially to the solution of this enigma that the Jew, Jesus, is central in the Christian religion and was for centuries almost totally ignored in Jewish hearts and Jewish minds, this as the result of persecution.

Contributing to the enigma have been the inevitable partisanships, some of which have spilled over into scholarship.

From time to time some Christian scholar writing of the period
of early Christianity has described a Judaism defaced by
superficial doctrines of reward and punishment and bogged
down in a narrow legalism that deprived the religion of heart.
This, of course, is a distortion, and the fact that such distortion
could come even from scholars is a testimony to human limita-
tions. On the other hand, there have been Jewish students who
have been willing to be exposed to the literature of the New
Testament but have shunned the profound and worthy scholarship of generations of Christian scholars. Some such Jewish
scholars have been marked by a condescension toward and disdain for Christianity corresponding to the academic disdain for
Judaism on the part of Christian scholars. In sum, then, scholarship has hitherto not provided any solution for this first and
great enigma.

The second enigma is the Holocaust, the destruction by
Hitler of virtually all of European Jewry except that of Britain
and Russia. As more than one Christian scholar has pointed
out, the Nazis who executed Hitler's demands were born Christians or were even still nominally Christian; indeed, facets of
the organized Evangelical Church in Germany capitulated to
Nazism. What has been most puzzling about the Holocaust
has been that Christian persecution of Jews had ceased in
Western civilization in the nineteenth century; sporadic incidents outside the West—such as the pogroms in Damascus in
1842, the celebrated Mortara affair of 1859 (a nursemaid had
the Mortara baby baptized in order to save its soul, and there-
upon the Church took the baby away from its parents), the pogroms in Russia in the 1880s and 1900s—called forth from
many parts of the Christian community protests against the
harm done to Jews. Large portions of the Christian community
arose to defend and assist Jews. The roots of Nazism lie, of
course, in the quasi-racial theories that arose in the 1870s, and
surely the Dreyfus affair of 1896 was a product more of such

racism than of specifically Christian hostility. Granted that in
the general populace there abided the folklore disdain of Jews,
by and large in the circles of educated and cultured people
Christian anti-Semitism had given way to Christian philo-
Semitism. In the world of biblical scholarship, denominational
lines were being overcome so that Christian and Jewish
scholars were beginning to read each other's books and to inau-
gurate an academic exchange that aggrandized both Christian
and Jewish scholarship.

Had there not been this record of Christian philo-Semitism
and had not religious persecution disappeared from the Western world, the Holocaust could have been expected. Instead,
the Holocaust is a refutation and rejection of much of the best
that the Western world has given its allegiance to.

It is not too difficult to set forth that Christian anti-
Semitism had paved the way for Nazi anti-Semitism, as many
scholars have done. Nevertheless, there remains an enigmatic
quality to the whole thing. How could those ordinary Germans
who were reared on the notion that the great theme of Christianity is love do as Nazis what they scarcely would have done as
Christians?

In the American scene Christian-Jewish relations in the nineteenth and twentieth centuries were free of the dreadful legacy
that marked Europe. There are no American streets with the
name Street of the Burning of the Jews; there is no American
counterpart to Little Hugh of Lincoln, whose death, ascribed
to Jews in that section of England, led to mass murders. In
America there was no physical ghetto. Jews and Christians at-
tended the same public schools and universities. In periods of
warfare American Jews and Christians served next to each
other in the Army and the Navy, and Jewish and Christian
chaplains found a common denominator in their common responsibilities to the Armed Forces. In the civilian world rabbis
and ministers exchanged pulpits. Jewish and Christian scholars

in the field of Bible met together in the Society of Biblical Literature and other academic organizations.

At no time in past history has there existed such amity between Jews and Christians as has developed in the United States. In Holland there has been much of this and in Britain a good bit, but in neither country has there been the quantity and depth that has marked the United States (and Canada). Accordingly, it is no longer surprising to find American Christians sympathetic to and becoming learned in Judaism, and American Jews studying the sacred Scripture and other documents of Christians.

I do not want to overpaint the scene. Let it be conceded that there are sections of Christendom in the United States and sections of Jewry that must be excepted from the account of these gratifying processes. Nevertheless, the relations between Jews and Christians in the United States have refuted most of the past history of relations of the two religions. A French scholar, Joseph Bonsirven, writing in 1936 on the topic of "The Jews and Jesus," noted with what frequency American rabbis speak from the pulpit on Jesus and asked somewhat wryly whether they ever spoke on other topics. (It was Bonsirven's lament that Jews were reclaiming Jesus for themselves but not bringing themselves to the Christ.)

*   *   *

What of Christian-Jewish relations in Israel? In the Zionist background of Israel there lay two impulses. The affirmative aspect was the place of Zion in the hopes and prayers of Jews, and the centrality of the hope of the return to the holy land in the traditional Jewish theology. On the other hand, the negative aspect in that background was the frustration of the hopes of Jews for emancipation, for the acquisition of civil rights and economic opportunity. While some Israelis represent a migration to the Holy Land that precedes in time the Nazi Holo-

caust, most adult Israelis are refugees from oppressions and persecutions suffered at the hands of nominal Christians in
Europe. What, then, have Jewish-Christian relations since the
establishment of the State of Israel been? In a setting so completely different from that of America, has there been reflected
in Israel anything similar, or widely dissimilar, or what? The
portrayal of such developments in Israel is the main topic of
this book. Surely anyone interested in the unfolding Christian-
Jewish relations in our time should be interested in this
firsthand report offered us by an Israeli observer, Pinchas Lapide.

There is one additional service that Dr. Lapide renders. All
too often the Jewish side of the Christian-Jewish controversy
has rested on the hostility of the Middle Ages and on the folklore among Jews about Christians (which balances the folklore
among Christians about Jews). In the Jewish folklore, Christians are guilty of illiteracy, stupidity, drunkenness, and a glorying in personal physical power, not in the power of the mind. A
contrary viewpoint, expressed by great Jewish sages and philosophers, has usually gone ignored. I do provide one example of
this other aspect of the Jewish response to Christianity in my
Anti-Semitism in the New Testament? Dr. Lapide, however,
provides many examples and it is wonderful to have this material brought together and presented so well.

Dr. Lapide first came to my attention with his inquiry into
the relations between recent popes and the Jews, wherein he
wanted to set straight the usual impression, both among Jews
and among Christians, that the papacy was totally unconcerned
for Jewish suffering. Dr. Lapide's book *The Pope and the Jews*,
based on archives at the Vatican, was a good corrective to
superficial and ill-based impressions.

I think that I should, in all honesty, issue a very quiet academic disclaimer about some of the passages in the book. One
in particular I must advert to—namely, Lapide's excessive cer-

tainty that there was a Hebrew version of some of the gospel
material. I think this is incorrect, and I regard it a legendary development from the view of the second-century Bishop Papias,
quoted in Eusebius, that Matthew had written his Gospel in
Hebrew. But this pedantic reservation is of no consequence.

The important thing is that Dr. Lapide has written an
enlightening book that ought to be of great interest to American Jews and Christians.

SAMUEL SANDMEL

Israelis, Jews,
and Jesus

In Lieu of an Introduction

There are three reasons why dialogue these days between Christians and Jews is both more urgent and more promising than ever:

First, because genuine, candid dialogue between the brothers of Jesus and his disciples has never yet taken place. At the time of the original schism, when the Church of the Gentiles broke away from its Jewish mother, members of both groups shouted at and abused one another with all the passion of quarrelling brothers. Later they pronounced one another heretics, and bound up their weal with the others' woe. Thanks to a general lack of faith, believers in the other camp were cursed as unbelievers, until finally their so-called disputations mirrored the tragic prototype of Cain and Abel: The question not *who* loved God more but *whom* (supposedly) God loved more became grounds for a conflict leading to fratricide. And last of all came silence, or talk of trivialities, not of the things that really mattered. Since "the others" were predestined to damnation anyway, and since everybody already knew all the answers to questions about God, conversation was useless.

Second, because in our day believing Jews and Christians

have become two islands in a sea of apathy, materialism, and atheism—a sea which grows ever more stormy and threatens to inundate them both.

Third, because we Jews and Christians are joined in brotherhood at the deepest level, so deep in fact that we have overlooked it and missed the forest of brotherhood for the trees of theology. We have an intellectual and spiritual kinship which goes deeper than dogmatics, hermeneutics, and exegesis. We are brothers in a manifold "elective affinity"

—in the belief in one God our Father,
—in the hope of His salvation,
—in ignorance of His ways,
—in humility before His omnipotence,
—in the knowledge that we belong to Him, not He to us,
—in love and reverence for God,
—in doubt about our wavering fidelity,
—in the paradox that we are dust and yet the image of God,
—in the consciousness that God wants us as partners in the sanctification of the world,
—in the condemnation of arrogant religious chauvinism,
—in the conviction that love of God is crippled without love of neighbor,
—in the knowledge that all speech about God must remain a stammering on our way to Him.

This book is dedicated to true dialogue, in which no one is "right," no one wins or converts the other, but each side listens and learns from the other.

I

Jesus in Hebrew Literature

The earliest writing about Jesus was composed in Hebrew and appeared, most probably, in Jerusalem. It was a collection of sayings which perhaps one of his disciples wished to record to guard them from the possible distortions of oral tradition. Or it may have been a protogospel designed to make the glad tidings of the rabbi of Nazareth accessible to all his fellow believers. We do not know for sure.

It is certain, however, that all four Greek Gospels display distinct traces of an original Hebrew text in their vocabulary, grammar, syntax, and semantic patterns. Hence we cannot seriously question the existence of a "Hebrew gospel"—no fewer than ten Fathers of the Church testify to it.[1]

But after this we must wait till the twentieth century for more Hebrew literature about Jesus, written in the same land of Israel, by the descendants of the same sons of Israel who

1. Papias (Eusebius, *Hist. Eccl.* III, 39, 1); Irenaeus (*ibid.*, V, 8, 2); Hegesippus (*ibid.*, IV, 22, 4); Jerome (*Contra Rufinum* VII, 77; *De vir. ill.* II; *In Matt.* 6, 11; *In Ezech.* 18, 7; *Adv. Pel.* III, 2 et al.); Origen (*In Matt.* XV, 14); Epiphanius (*Panarion* I, 29, 7 and 9); Theodoret of Cyprus (*Haer. Fab.* II, 1); Nicephorus Callistus (*Eccl. Hist.* III, 13); Clement of Alexandria (*Strom.* II, IX, 45, 5); Pantaenus (Eusebius, *ibid.*, V, 10, 3).

made up the original audience of all the sermons of the Nazarene. What happened in the almost two thousand years between these two epochs takes up a vast chapter in the history
of the world. This period saw the transformation of a Jewish
"way" into a sect composed of Jews and Gentiles and finally a
Church of Gentiles embracing the entire world. Its history is an
unparalleled record of blood and suffering, and at its beginning
stands that rabbi from Nazareth who bled on the cross and rose
from the dead—a symbol for all Israel which was tormented
and jeered, hated and murdered, only to rise again in our days
in the place where it first became the people of the Bible.

The laureate of modern Hebrew poetry Chaim Nachman
Bialik (1873–1934) did not see Jesus in the customary theolog-
ical light but assigned to him a key role in his overview of the
Jewish salvation history on which he bases his Zionist credo:
"This country has been blessed with a special gift to transform
little things into great at the eleventh hour. Around four thousand years ago bands of nomadic herdsmen gathered here from
Ur in Chaldea, Aram, Egypt, and the West Arabian wilderness.
Out of them grew . . . a little nation, poor and needy at that
time—the people of Israel. . . . Within it arose simple men,
sheep breeders, farmers, and settlers like their brothers, who
bore the storm of the divine spirit in their hearts and God's
thunder and roar on their lips. These humble men, who spoke
to rulers and peoples about the story of their times and the
daily cares of man, dared to lift their eyes to eternity, to heaven
and the universe. They were the ones, ultimately, who gave the
world the foundations of faith and an ethical civilization.
Down through hundreds of generations, over the heads of nations who mounted the stage of the world and then left it,
their voice still reaches us. It rings out today, through the almighty power of God, stronger, grander, and more sonorous
than ever before. . . . After the proclamation of Cyrus, exiles
by the tens of thousands returned and went up to this barren

land. Again they became a little, wretched community, smaller and poorer than the first. Barely five centuries went by, when another Jew arose in this little country, the son of an Israelite carpenter, who brought the message of redemption to the Gentile world, to prepare the way for the days of the Messiah. . . . Two thousand years have passed since then, but the idols have not yet retreated from the face of the earth. Then came the Balfour Declaration, and for the third time Israel has gathered in its own land. Not for nothing has the hand of God led this people for four thousand years through all the pains of hell to bring it back now for the third time into this land."[2]

The first Hebrew book on Jesus in modern times came from the pen of a well-known Jewish historian, Joseph Klausner, who wrote it mainly for his students at the Hebrew University in Jerusalem.[3] "If I were to succeed," he wrote in the foreword to the first edition, "in conveying to the Hebrew reader a factual picture of the historical Jesus, different from the portrayal in Christian as well as Jewish theology, and, as far as possible, objective and scientific . . . if I succeed in this, I may be allowed to claim to have covered a page in the history of Israel which has hitherto been written almost exclusively by Christians."

Klausner stresses above all the basically Jewish character of Jesus and his teaching: "In all his views and actions Jesus was a Jew. As a pious Israelite he fulfilled all the commandments. He saw in God his Father in heaven, had pity on the poor, supported the stumbling, and loved the repentant, in whose place even the perfectly just are not allowed to stand, as a talmudic saying puts it. He was also afflicted with the typical Jewish failings. He never saw the sublime and beautiful in nature, and he never smiled. He carried on his teaching amid tears, threats,

2. *Debarim Sheb'al Peh* (Tel Aviv, 1935), I, 55.
3. *Yeshu Ha-notzri* (Jerusalem, 1922); *Jesus of Nazareth*, trans. Herbert Danby (New York: Macmillan, 1925).

and promises. . . . Jesus was the most Jewish of all Jews, more Jewish even than the great teacher Hillel."

Klausner sees Jesus' particular strength in his ethics, whose basic elements are already to be found in Jewish tradition: "There is not one ethical concept in the Gospels which cannot be traced back to Moses and the prophets. Does that rob Jesus of all originality? By no means! Jesus' peculiar contribution lay in his extending the biblical ethos all the way to Utopia, in his one-sided stressing of morality over law [Halakah], in his general overemphasis on morals, which consciously crowds the social environment into the background, neglects the people, and conjures up the danger of categorical imperatives lapsing into fanaticism. Judaism is not just a religion and not just ethics but the sum of all a people's needs resting as a whole on a religious foundation—in other words a national world view on a religious-ethical basis."

The excessive demands which Jesus makes of human nature —the norms which only angels can fulfill—find their deplorable counterpart in Christian practice. "Where do we find there the meekness, forgiveness seventy seven times, love of enemies, and turning the other cheek?" Klausner asks, and his question has been tested by centuries of suffering. He concludes, inevitably, "Jesus' teachings and his history have never become a part of Israel, but for the rest of the world's people he has been 'a light for the Gentiles.' "

Klausner offers the following opinion on Jesus' sense of himself: "Jesus was convinced that he was the Messiah, there can be no doubt of that. Otherwise he would have been nothing more than an evil impostor and deceiver. He would never have been able to influence world history nor to bring a new religion into life, which has lasted for almost two thousand years." Still this has nothing to do with the divinization of Jesus, for, as the Nazarene knew, "Even the Jewish Messiah is only a mortal man among his fellows. . . . Only God can truly redeem. The

Messiah is simply His chosen instrument for realizing the plan of salvation."

And yet it is hard for Klausner to renounce Jesus entirely. In the last chapter of his work we read, "If the day should ever come when the ethical code of the Nazarene is stripped of the mythology, miracles, and mysticism which veil it, then Jesus' 'Book of Ethics' will become one of the most precious treasures in the literature of Israel."

* * *

Many of the Jewish pioneers from Eastern Europe, who came from little village communities in Poland or the Ukraine to build the Jewish state in the land of the Bible, knew Jesus only as a wooden crucifix at a wayside shrine or a crossroads. Thus Isaac Dov Berkowitz (1885–1961) writes in his *Childhood Memories*[4] about a crucifix which stood on the way to the synagogue. "All Jewish children were strictly ordered to turn completely away from it, and on no account to pollute their eyes with the idol. . . . One day I could no longer resist the temptation. When I got to the dangerous place, I took my life in my hands, turned around, and looked up at the naked figure of a man on the cross. The impression was . . . uncanny, terrifying in its strangeness. I saw the tired head drooping on the pale shoulders, the loins wrapped in a cloth, the thin legs hanging limply down, closed eyes that had forgotten life and no longer saw the light. I gazed full of wonder: what could it mean? Is that him? . . . But then along came a farmer on his horsecart, stopped, and crossed himself. When he saw me standing there, his face darkened, he uttered a curse, and cracked his whip at me. I ran away as fast as I could, pursued by a mysterious fear."

Hitler's genocide has affected the image of Jesus in four ways:

4. Tel Aviv, 1965.

—As a counterpoise to the sea of tears from Auschwitz, people sought refuge in a factual, scientific image of the Nazarene, beyond passions and emotions.

—The figure of Christ was humanized, avoiding both the deification of the Christian churches and the diabolization of the sort that occurs in the lampoons of the Jewish Middle Ages. These authors are seeking neither the gospel Son of God nor the Talmud's heretic and perverter of the people but the human brother who lived an exemplary Jewish life in a world full of inhumanity.

—Nevertheless, here and there in Israeli literature we find the antithesis to this "brother Jesus." Just as all too many Christians still associate "Judaism" with "Judas," many survivors of the "final solution" cannot separate Christ from the Christendom that committed or tolerated the murder of six million Jews. Their caricature often borders on hatred of Christ— although at bottom this is only a literary reaction to the trauma caused by wholesale slaughter.

—But on the whole we are dealing with the process of the Jewish recovery of Jesus, of bringing him home. This inscribes his name, with the honor due a hero, on the mass graves of the victims of Nazism or in the ranks of the resistance fighters. The faith and zeal of the Nazarene, the unshakable power of his hope, the deep love which he cherished for Israel, and his tragic death have made him dear to many thinkers and poets in Israel today, beyond all walls and graves.

All these approaches have in common a growing sympathy for the life and death of the Galilean, a feeling often indistinguishable from love, and a consciousness, evident even in writings hostile to Christ, of sharing as brothers in a common fate. Typical of the "anti-Jesus school," for whom Auschwitz forms the link between the cross and the swastika is the Israeli writer Shin Shalom (1904–73), who writes in his *Galilean*

Journal,[5] "I know Galilee the way a man knows his own soul. I know its wild rocky gorges, its hidden springs, its vast, clear skies . . . but there is a man in Galilee whom I know nothing about, whom I have never asked after. His existence is for me an open wound, which no one touches, which one tries *not* to think about. Quiet! Just don't remind me of it. . . . When I was in that menacing mountain range called Nazareth and thought I saw his eyebrows wrinkled in pain, I closed my eyes. I would not let his name cross my lips. I did not curse, I did not bless. I said nothing. . . . But sometimes a voice came up out of the silence, the voice of a lost brother, the voice of a man who has gone off course, has gone astray among strangers, who at the same time confesses his guilt and points an accusing finger, who wants to come back, if you'll go out to meet him lovingly and whisper only one word in his ear: brother! In that hour I mustered all my support troops—all the bitter memories of my life and all the terrible experiences in the history of my people—lest this man clear himself before me by his confession. Out of the abyss of oblivion I brought up all the tortures of the Inquisition, all the butchery of the pogroms, all the murders of the holy crusades, all the blows which we suffer from the bearers of his name, all the outrage we have had to endure from the guardians of his teaching. The endless chain of the generations of tortured martyrs, the armies of Jewish brothers wandering restlessly around, despised, hunted and hounded from prison to prison, from atrocity to atrocity—I had to make them all march up in a broad front against him, to force him to silence, to make him keep to himself, to push him away from me with both hands—this one-time brother, the carpenter's son from Galilee."

*   *   *

5. German edition, Heidelberg, 1954.

André Schwarz-Bart, a young French Jew who lost his family in
the gas chambers, raises in his novel *The Last of the Just* a me-
morial for all Jewish martyrs. This masterpiece, which won its
author the Jerusalem Prize in 1967, was immediately translated
into Hebrew (and fourteen other languages) and is still an
influential book in Israel. Here is a conversation between two
doomed young Jews, Ernie and his fiancee Golda:

"'Oh, Ernie,' Golda said, 'you know them. Tell me why,
why do the Christians hate us the way they do? They seem so
nice when I can look at them without my star.'

"Ernie put his arm around her shoulders solemnly. 'It's very
mysterious,' he murmured in Yiddish. 'They don't know exactly why themselves. I've been in their churches and I've read
their gospel. Do you know who the Christ was? A simple Jew
like your father. A kind of Hasid.'

"Golda smiled gently. 'You're kidding me.'

"'No, no, believe me, and I'll bet they'd have got along fine,
the two of them, because he was really a good Jew, you know,
sort of like the Baal Shem Tov. . . . The Christians say they
love him, but I think they hate him without knowing it. So
they take the cross by the other end and make a sword out of it
and strike us with it! You understand, Golda,' he cried suddenly, strangely excited, *they take the cross and they turn it
around, my God. . . .*'

"'Poor Jesus, if he came back to earth and saw that the pagans had made a sword out of him and used it against his
sisters and brothers, he'd be sad, he'd grieve forever. . . .'

"'Yes, maybe he sees it. They say that some of the Just Men
remain outside the gates of Paradise, that they don't want to
forget humanity, that they too await the Messiah. . . . Who
knows? You understand, Goldeleh, he was a little old-fashioned
Jew, a real Just Man, you know, no more nor no less than . . .
all our Just Men.' "[6]

6. Tr. Stephen Becker (New York: Atheneum, 1960), pp. 323–24.

*   *   *

At first glance the ballad "The Last Words of Don Henriques"
seems to be simply the swan song of a famous victim of the
Spanish Inquisition. But anyone who reads this poem by Salman Shneur (1887–1959) a second time will hear in it the
pounding pulse of the most recent Jewish Passion. The first
strophe laconically describes the situation:

> The words of Don Henriques
> in flames at the stake,
> as a crucifix of the Savior
> sways in the wind before him.

The noble Marrano, who had accepted baptism to escape
death, is condemned to the stake when he is caught in the act
of reciting a Jewish prayer. He senses in the crucified form of
Jesus which a Dominican holds out to him a true companion
in suffering:

> "Oh man of Nazareth,
> Jesus, my good brother,
> Don't trust the Gentiles, my Jesus,
> I've tasted their deceit to the dregs. . . .
> Soon the day will come
> when they chase you
> from their lands, from their church steeples,
> from the necks of their wives and children,
> like a dog they'll trample you down,
> throw you out of their splendid churches,
> built by Copts, Byzantines, and Goths
> to glorify your name. . . .
> Peoples and tongues will regret it,
> in shame they will cover their faces,
> beat their breasts in repentance,
> loudly confess they have sinned
> by turning a Jew into God,
> to pay homage to him
> through thirty generations.

'Out you go!' they will scream,
the way they always have.
'You have deceived us, you Jew!
For the price of a wooden cross
you've bought the fame of Zeus and Odin!
To the stake with you, Marranos!'
The self-same fate awaits us both,
today it's the turn of Henriques,
soon you'll be there, my Jesus. . . ."

As the flames climb higher, the feverish eyes of the crypto-
Jew gaze on an endless procession of figures dressed in rags, pilgrims trudging to the East—the exodus of all Jewish martyrs
from the mass graves of the Diaspora to the promised land. At
their head marches the Nazarene:

"Mothers, wives, and sisters,
all the true daughters of Israel,
dressed in white and black,
will stand along the way
to honor the exiles.
In you and the thousands,
the tens of thousands of figures
they will recognize once more
every mother her only son,
tormented and tortured to death,
every wife her husband,
whose tongue was ripped from his throat,
every sister discovers her brother,
slaughtered in numberless pogroms,
and every orphan his lifeless father. . . .
Oh you endless chain of Golgothas
from Europe all the way to Mount Zion!"

The poet demands the recovery of Jesus from his alienation
among the Gentiles (the biblical metaphor compares it with

leprosy), followed by the vindication of his honor in an independent Israel:

> "And you, noble companion in pain,
> striding in front of them all,
> a new Sanhedrin bids you welcome,
> wrapped in new prayer shawls,
> they'll lead you to the Jordan,
> wash you clean in its holy water,
> bathe your wounds and heal them,
> to lighten your tear-darkened eyes,
> to cleanse you from Gentile impurity,
> from their sacrifices and incense,
> and from the soot of the Torah rolls that they
>   burned. . . .
> Cleansed, recovered, and pure,
> like Namaan, commander of the armies of Aram,[7]
> they'll greet you with jubilation. . . .
> with open arms and hearts full of love . . .
> a penitent brother come home.
>
> No Pilate will have the power in Israel
> to pass a bloody Roman sentence,
> for the land is ours
> and ours the verdict of justice.
> No stranger will then
> dare to sit in judgment
> on a dispute between brothers. . . ."

And so Don Henriques dies, like countless fellow believers of his, with the words of the Jewish confession of faith on his lips:

> "O Jesus, my brother from Nazareth,
> I am breathing my last. . . .
> Lift me up, thou God of Jacob,
> set me on fire high above the multitude!

7. Cf. 2 Kings 5:3–14.

I have been blessed
beyond the lot of other mortals,
and so I will praise the name of God,
Praised be our Creator,
who made me a torch to guide the erring. . . .
Listen to me, nations,
hear, yes, all of Israel, hear!
Cry out with me, Jesus, join with me and say:
Our Lord . . . our Lord . . . is One."[8]

Uri Zvi Greenberg (born 1894) calls his poetry "a science of
mourning and a religion of hope." More precisely, it is a mystical vision that sees in the full sovereignty of Israel the
fulfillment of biblical promises. He excludes Jesus from Christianity (which is for him the creation of Paul), so as to make a
clear distinction between the Galilean "school of Jesus" and
Roman Christianity. The first belongs to Judaism; the second
he calls "a foreign fruit cultivated by the Gentiles."

In a mystical elegy, "I Will Tell It to a Child,"[9] he identifies
himself with Jesus, in allegorical tones of messianic longing
which no translation can do justice to:

He didn't come, the Messiah . . . like an eagle
he wheeled high over the bloody abyss.
Day and night I heard the beating of his wings,
on Jaffa's coast he landed in the form of a man . . .
Poor and humble, yet mighty in the strength of a seer.
A sword he bore up to Jerusalem. . . .
He came so near . . . here he stood . . . but he only
reached the city's edge, the threshold of the kingdom.
There he cast out the shopkeepers . . . who greeted him
with scorn and denials—the shopkeepers . . .
when they had finished chatting,
laughed out loud: Hahaha—the Messiah turned away
as if stabbed by a dagger.

8. Tel Aviv: Am Oved, 1952, pp. 394–400.
9. *Book of Accusation and Faith* (Tel Aviv, 1937).

I too turned, as if struck with a dagger,
Thus the shopkeepers vanquished him . . .

And I heard him ask with bleeding lips:
Where are the generations that waited for me,
who called me from Rome
to the threshold of fame?
And I heard his last word:
Woe is me, woe unto you, my homeland . . .
and the Messiah turned his face and went on his way. . . .
Where he went, I don't know; I cannot know,
perhaps he went inside me,
and I nourish him with my flesh,
and slake his thirst with blood, sweeter than wine . . .
perhaps not . . . perhaps he was the one I saw
shaped like an eagle, wheeling high over the Kidron valley,
slowly wheeling, over the Temple, sobbing . . .
Israel's redeemer, birdlike, bidding farewell
to the Holy Temple Mount.
And again he dipped invisibly
into the fountain of Hebrew blood,
shackled for two thousand years,
obeying the Messiah's law,
a second time, for two millennia,
who knows?

"In the Name of Rabbi Jesus of Nazareth"[10] is the title of a
short story by Avigdor Hameiri (1886–1970) which the writer
claimed was based on an actual experience. A troop of Hungarian soldiers, under the author's command, was taken prisoner in the First World War by a company of Russians. As
soon as the Russian officer realized that most of his prisoners
were Jews, he decided, in between two bottles of vodka, to "do
divine justice" to them. After a court martial, frequently interrupted by drunken shouts, belching, and curses, the czar's lieu-

10. Tel Aviv: Massada, 1944.

tenant informed his prisoners, "You're fully aware of the charge. . . . It has now been decided to repay you tit for tat. Since you're in the habit of drinking Christian blood, it's high time you got to taste Jewish blood for a change. Therefore one of you is condemned to drink Jewish blood. Secondly, you crucified the Son of God. Therefore, one of you will now be crucified. Thirdly, one of you will be buried alive, just as Jesus was buried before he arose on the third day. Is that clear?"

This "sentence" was carried out "in the name of Rabbi Jesus of Nazareth." The author, who had been picked to be buried alive, was the last in line. As the Russians began to fill up his trench with clumps of earth, they were interrupted by a Hungarian counterattack, which left the self-appointed dispenser of "divine justice" dead and the gravediggers decamping as fast as possible, while the author lived to see his own resurrection. The improvised grave, it turned out, had saved him from the bullets of his liberators. This horrible story aims at revealing the abyss between Jesus' commandment of love and the twisted travesty of hatred which many "Christians" make of it.

*   *   *

Samuel Joseph Agnon (1888–1970), Israel's winner of the Nobel Prize for Literature (1966), is today a classic author whose works are required reading in all the schools of Israel. With his Hasidic origins and his Orthodox way of life, he made religion the leitmotif of most of his works. At the state banquet given in his honor at Stockholm when he was awarded the Nobel Prize, he said to his Swedish hosts, "My writing has been influenced principally by the Bible, the Mishnah, and the Talmud. Then come the medieval exegetes of the Halakah as well as Hebrew poets and philosophers, above all Maimonides. . . ." And like all believing Jews he closed his speech with the expression of a messianic hope: "May the redeemer come soon to Zion, to fill the earth with the knowledge of God, to

the joy of all dwellers on earth, and let them be granted peace
and harmony in abundance!"

With this in mind it is all the more astonishing that Agnon
devoted an enigmatic short story to the figure of Jesus, under
the biblical title "Paths of Righteousness" (cf. Ps 23:3). Although he does not mention Jesus by name but makes use of
the old rabbinical paraphrase "that man," the context leaves no
doubt about the identity of the central figure. The story describes the bitter fate of an old Polish Jew, a vinegar maker,
whose family has died and whose life is withering emptily
away. He has only one remaining desire, to spend the rest of his
days in the Holy Land, where he hopes to be buried. In order
to reach this ardently longed-for goal, every day he saves a few
kopecks by cutting down on food. He fasts twice a week, and
three times he works long overtime hours, all to scrape together
the fare.

"And on the evening before each Sabbath, after he had sold
his vinegar and returned home from the city, he sat down on a
stone, counted his takings, and divided them into two little
piles of coins. One of them he slipped into his trouser pocket
for the bodily needs of the coming week, the other he put in
the poor box which the Gentiles in that country had fastened
between the hands of 'that man' at the crossroad. He was simple and had no idea what purpose the box was supposed to
serve, but he thought in his heart that he could find no surer
place for his savings. . . ."

Thus several years passed by, with continual hard work, on
the edge of starvation, but filled with high hopes. One day
when his nest egg had reached the sum needed to book passage,
he flew to the wooden cross halfway to the city, took a pointed
stone, and got ready to break open his savings bank. But as
chance would have it, that very day some priests had arrived
from Rome to collect the offerings. They found him in front of
the crucifix with a stone in his hand. So he was arrested and

thrown into prison . . . and the whole city simmered like a witches' cauldron.

Some days later he was brought in chains into the hall of judgment. "The judge asked him, 'Do you admit that you were caught trying to break open the box?' The old man answered, 'I wanted to open the box, because the money . . .' The judge didn't let him finish, but broke in hoarsely, 'The defendant has confessed his crime!' Unable to explain either the circumstances or his motives, the defendant listened spellbound as the priests confirmed his deposition.

" 'That's witchcraft,' he thought in his heart. 'They all speak the truth, but the truth doesn't lead to a just judgment.' He looked down at his chains and then up over the head of his judge. Suddenly his roving eye found the form of 'that man' hanging on the wall of the courtroom. . . . Half to himself he said, 'So, you're laughing at me?' With both his hands he struck the wooden balustrade in front of him till the rattling of the iron chains echoed through the whole courtroom. 'Let me go free, and give me my money back!' he cried out. They beat him and led him back to his cell. There he prayed all alone in the darkness: 'Master of the universe, thou knowest how long I have suffered in exile, how little I've eaten, what rags I wear, how my life was sourer than the vinegar I support myself with —all this, just to get to thy Holy Land. . . .' "

When he had finally prayed himself to sleep, "The door of the prison opened and one in the form of a man [the Hebrew means "a son of man"] appeared, a box between his hands; a strange smile played on his lips. The old man turned his glance away and tried to go back to sleep. But 'that man' bade him arise and said to him, 'Hold tight to me and I'll bring you where you want to go.' . . . The old man stretched his arms out to 'that man' and stammered, 'How can I do that with chains on my hands?' But he said, 'Try it anyway!' Then the old man stretched both hands out and clung to the neck of 'that man,' and 'that man' smiled as he said to him, 'This very day I will bring you to the land of Israel.' . . . But in the middle of the flight the old man felt that he had nestled up against a cold stone. His heart stood still, and his arms went limp. He lost his footing and fell to the ground. The next morning when the prison guards entered his cell, it was empty. But during the very same night a knock was heard on the door of a synagogue in Jerusalem. When they opened up, they saw a group of messengers [band of angels[11]] who had come from the Diaspora and were carrying a shape which resembled a man. Without a sound they washed the dead man and buried him just before daybreak, for no corpse may linger in the Holy City overnight."[12]

This story fits into the genre of those miracle tales so frequent in the corpus of Jewish legends. This time Jesus plays the role which rabbinical legends have ascribed since ancient times to a different figure, Elijah the prophet, who saves Jews from danger and distress as a reward for their faith. The contradiction between the disparaging anonymity of "that man" (a holdover from medieval polemics) and the hero's role played here by Jesus is characteristic not only of Agnon but also of the gradual rethinking of Jesus in the ranks of the older generation of Hebrew writers in Israel.

One member of this generation was Chaim Hasas (1897–1973), who was elected an honorary citizen of Jerusalem and president of the Israeli Writers Union. He was a master of word painting, who brought his knowledge of all areas of Hebrew literature into play and still wrote in a distinctly personal style. One of his famous short stories, whose title, freely translated, reads "That's the Way the Goyim Are,"[13]

11. Both translations fit the Hebrew.
12. *Elu Va'elu* (Tel Aviv: Schocken, 1960), pp. 380–88.
13. "Elu Hem," in the yearbook of the newspaper *Davar* (Tel Aviv, 1946), pp. 16–21.

is written in the Mishnaic Hebrew which was spoken in Jesus' lifetime. He begins with an adaptation of the Synoptic
accounts of Jesus, in which he gives free rein to poetic license.
Thus, for example, in the temptation scene the devil is demythologized in good Jewish fashion into a "bad impulse," but
still remains enough of a real individual to try his best to talk
Jesus out of his mission to the Jews.

"But surely you know that Israel will never accept your
teaching or listen to you—stubborn and headstrong as they
are." When Jesus wraps himself in silence, the bad impulse
goes on, "Why must you fritter away your energies on this
spoiled people? Their death sentence is already signed and
sealed. If you want to succeed, knock on the door of the Gentiles, who will gladly bid you welcome." After a short but
pointed exchange of views, Jesus reveals his determination: "I
would rather die! I shall bear my cross, but I shall never commit such an outrage. My Father in heaven has sent me to his
children, the people of Israel. . . . In comparison with them
the Gentiles count for nothing."

After upbraiding the Gentiles in a speech which has various
parallels in the New Testament,[14] Jesus goes on to cry out in
indignation, in words which every Jewish soul might have spoken after the Second World War: "The doctrine which I came
to preach is a way to perfection; a commandment of love and
grace, of mercy and justice, a doctrine of humility, forgiveness,
and repentance. No one else outside of Israel can fulfill it, for
their forefathers stood on Mount Sinai and received the first
commandments. . . . These Gentiles, who want to have nothing to do with Sinai, revel in idolatry and superstition; they are
cruel by nature; they thirst after power—no, my teaching is not
for them, not for them. . . ."

To which the bad impulse deviously replies, "If this is what

14. E.g., Mt 7:6; 10:5; 15:26; Mk 7:27.

you want, keep your teaching to yourself or bury it deep in the
earth. . . . Otherwise the Gentiles will come, thieves that they
are, and take it away from you. After all, they steal everything
that tempts their ears and eyes." After Jesus has overcome the
bad impulse, he is granted a vision of Israel's odyssey of pain.

". . . He saw the destruction of the Temple, and how the
sons of Israel were dragged off as captives into exile. Moments
later the Roman Empire, mother of atrocities, split up before
his eyes into rival kingdoms. Still quivering like pieces of a
mangled snake, her cities filled up with houses of idolatry with
the figure of a crucified man nailed to their portals—and Israel
was hunted like an outlawed beast. Jesus was horrified by this
grisly figure on the cross, which caused innocent blood to be
shed and which became a thorn in Israel's flesh. While the
great stage of the world before him grew crowded with a terrible nightmare of murder, war, and anarchy, he tried to grasp
who this figure might be, what it wanted, and how it could
have been transformed with such lightning speed into an object
of pagan adoration. . . . Cities and states took up arms; armies
marched against one another, each bearing the wooden statue
of that crucified man in their vanguard. Meanwhile Israel, scattered in their midst, kept faith with its heavenly Father,
though its eyes with silent longing kept a lookout for the Redeemer: See there, he is coming, but no, not yet—and the peoples of the world mistreat the Jews, persecute and torture them,
with wanton bloodlust and malice. . . . And now an endless
procession assembles, knights and horsemen who close their
ranks to ride up to Jerusalem, the Holy City, to the grave of
their God, the cross sewn on their breast as an emblem. On the
way, they hurl themselves like a pack of hungry wolves on the
settlements of Israel, sowing rapine and murder wherever they
go. . . . Jews are torn out of their houses, thrown into the tem-
ples of idols, and forced down on their knees before that
crucified sovereign. For all that they go on praising their God,

they surrender their bodies and souls to glorify the name of their only Creator. . . . Jesus shook his head in wonder over these Gentiles, their blindness, and their delusion that God could die and have a grave in Jerusalem. . . . And his heart bled for his brothers, hunted to the ends of the earth, mocked by the Gentiles, and still praising God at the stake and in the torture chambers zealously prepared for them by thousands of priests and princes to test their strength of soul. . . . And look there, one of the Gentiles, at war with his brothers, counseled them to eradicate Israel once and for all, from the infant to the last old man, so that no remnant of their name should remain on God's broad earth. And it happened as he said: A blood-bath, an orgy of brutality was unleashed, such as no human eye had ever witnessed. . . . And then the Gentiles returned to their deeds of horror, while Israel, a miserable remnant, a handful of survivors, bleeding and half dead, left the lands of exile, shook the dust of the Diaspora from their feet, to seek refuge in the land of their fathers, a quiet harbor, safe from Gentile rage, for the last of the Jews. . . . A shiver seized Jesus at the sight of all these events, and then suddenly a dazzling light blinded his eyes. For a moment the wild hope gripped him that the Messiah had finally come to illumine the darkness of God. . . . He opened his eyes and looked hesitantly into the wilderness, awakening now with the first rays of the sun.

" 'What a dream I had tonight,' he murmured, still shuddering all over. 'And what is the meaning of the face that I saw?' " With a sigh of resignation Jesus arises and closes with the words to which the story owes its title: "That's the way the goyim are—till the end of time."

*   *   *

Early in 1968 a little ecumenical group of music lovers met each week in the Crusader Church of Abu Ghosh not far from Jerusalem, to play and sing J. S. Bach's *St. Matthew Passion*.

At first only a few critics paid any attention, commending the new initiative in the Sabbath supplement of two daily newspapers. But as soon as Bach's libretto was translated into Hebrew and young Israelis sang in Hebrew such fateful lines as "Crucify him!" and "His blood be upon us and upon our children!" the press began to call attention to the new "Bach ecumenism." Within a month a public controversy flared up, and it seemed in May 1968 as if the Abu Ghosh festival might be closed down by the police as a disturbance of the peace. That was more than the music lovers of Jerusalem were willing to suffer in silence. In their protest for Bach they at once got energetic support from a growing number of friends who took the field together in journalistic and parliamentary polemics for "musical freedom."

These commentators raised their voices not only to defend Bach and church music in Israel but to broaden the debate to include the New Testament. Typical of this group was J. Carmel (born 1901), whose essay "The Bach *Passion:* Yes or No?" was published at the time in *Keshet*,[15] one of the most influential literary quarterlies in Israel. Carmel wanted to contest the allegation that singing the verses from Matthew could help revive the idea of the murder of God. "None of the Jewish historians . . . deny Jewish responsibility. . . . In fact, Professor Klausner maintains that the Sadducees have a share in the blame. . . . Just as the Jews handed Jesus over to the Roman procurator of the country, since they had no jurisdiction over 'capital crimes,' so too the opponents of Rabbi Shneur Salman of Liadi handed him over to the Russian authorities.[16] . . . If Jesus' crucifixion was a part of the plan of salvation, then the Jews were only playing their predestined role. And if God for unfathomable reasons led them to commit this exalted crime, in order to rec-

15. Tel Aviv, Spring 1973, pp. 46–63.
16. In 1806.

oncile mankind . . . then we deserve indulgence, pity, and love
—and all of Christianity's offences against us remain unforgiva-
ble, till Israel one day finds redemption. . . . We did that
deed, but I feel no guilt because of it. Therefore I am free to
deal critically with the Gospels, as with any other great book
that has stamped its seal on world history."

Carmel regrets that the Gospels have not been given a permanent place in the Jewish literature section of all Israeli cur-
ricula. "My heart bled over the loss [in the schools] of this
tragic yet so tender book, so lovable and warm in its closeness
to life. Alien? I felt no alienation reading it. . . . Its native soil
is our own land. If the prophet Elijah rode to heaven in a
flaming chariot, why shouldn't Jesus rise from the dead and ascend into heaven? And, as in the case of Elijah, here too it is
not the supernatural but the human, all too human, which gives
wings to head and heart. Just as the figure of Elijah and his life
story lose nothing of their pathos even when we have ceased to
believe in his ascent into heaven, so Jesus and his story of
suffering are in no way diminished if we can believe neither in
his miraculous birth nor his resurrection. . . . Scenes like those
in Gethsemane, his agonizing prayer, the arrest at midnight, his
outcry on the cross . . . the masterworks of world literature
contain only a few such high points, such fateful moments."

Referring to Klausner's famous wish, "If the day should ever
come when the ethical code of the Nazarene is stripped of the
mythology, miracles, and mysticism which veil it, then Jesus'
'Book of Ethics' will become one of the most precious treasures
in the literature of Israel," Carmel poses the rhetorical question
"Has not this day already come? For us the veils have never
existed. And now, since they are beginning to fall away in the
domain of Christianity, what is still keeping us from passing on
this book to the Israeli reader? If Confucius and the Koran have
been translated into Hebrew . . . why not the New Testament,
with its deeper and more human values? When I read the Gos-

pel of Matthew, I understand how easy it is to reinterpret this chronicle of the ancient past into a fully relevant life story which has much to say to us even today."

Carmel is, however, fully conscious of the historical implications of his proposal: "In the name of the gospel innumerable Jews have been murdered. Nobody will deny that. But we must not forget that every idea, every ideal, even the noblest and most universal, changes in the course of its development and is usually distorted both in form and substance—until finally it often degenerates into its antithesis."

Carmel strongly emphasizes that we can blame neither Jesus nor his disciples for this estrangement of Christianity from its true self, much less for the monstrous crimes which the churches have committed in the name of Jesus against his brothers. Lastly he dispels any suspicion that he intends to promote Christian missionary efforts among the Jews. "When I speak of the Gospels, it is without any view towards incorporating yet another holy book into our literature. I take no pleasure in a canon, with all the narrowness implied in such a concept. My only concerns are of a literary, cultural, and intellectual nature. . . . As a matter of fact, the Gospels are religious writings, and anyone who wishes to be influenced by them in a religious way should be free to do so. . . . There are people who derive religious insights from Dostoevsky. Others may react in a similar way to the Gospels. Why not? What are we afraid of? Or must we be anxious lest Jews once again look upon Jesus as Messiah and redeemer?"

* * *

While Carmel merely recommends introducing the New Testament, by way of excerpts, as required reading for the secondary schools in Israel, Salman Chen (born 1929), a typical representative of the younger sabra generation, goes a meaningful step farther. In his recent book *Ways to Heaven*[17] he writes, "The Christian question or Christianity question confronts the Jew in Israel at a time of social upheaval which makes almost all traditional values precarious, and of scientific revolution which enthrones pragmatic facts. . . . The theological aspect of the issue is of no concern to Jews and seems to touch fewer and fewer Christians as well. On the other hand, the question of Jesus' timeless contribution to better understanding of the universal human mission in world history is . . . very much a Jewish question in the state of Israel."

While Chen maintains his distance from the "all too lofty and largely rhetorical morality" of the Nazarene since it demands too much of people and thus has no practical normative value, another doctrine of Jesus does attract him: "A central idea in Jesus' teaching is the freeing of faith from every fetter of locality and ethnic origin. . . . The idea of a fully unconditional, unlimited freedom with which one professes an ideology or a belief has great, epoch-making value. . . . The way to God, according to Jesus, is through the faith of the heart and total, selfless love, not through the observance of difficult commandments in all their Pharisaic exactitude. . . . One is therefore allowed to pluck ears of wheat and heal the sick on the Sabbath. . . . This insight, which in its later extension gave Christianity its universal dimension, undoubtedly represents a substantial step forward. Here we find the realization of prophetic ideology on a sweeping scale. Judaism has yet to find the way to a similar universalization of its faith and life. . . . By insisting that man is lord of the Sabbath, Jesus pointed out a humane, social rationale rather than a ritual one for observing the Sabbath rest. . . . By stipulating, 'Not what goes into the mouth defiles a man, but what comes out of the mouth, this defiles a man,' he laid a new foundation for the dietary laws:

17. *Derachim Lashamayim* (Tel Aviv: Milo, 1972).

medical, moral, and aesthetic guidelines, instead of ta-
boos. . . . Jesus' position on all these questions is surely more
progressive than the rigid, harsh mentality of the Halakah
scribes. It is, in fact, the attitude of most Jews in Israel
today. . . . Such a rethinking of premises, characteristic of
Jesus' ideas on reform, is urgently needed, not only to adapt Judaism to the needs and demands of our age . . . but also to foster and increase contacts between Jews and the world around
them."

David Flusser, who points to the love of enemies as Jesus'
distinctive contribution, by which "Christianity surpasses Judaism, at least theoretically, in its approach of love to all men,"[18]
is also of the opinion that Jesus' message can be instructive for
contemporary Jews: "It will seem paradoxical to the Christian
that the Jew can learn from Jesus how to pray, the true sense of
the Sabbath, how to fast, the meaning of the kingdom of
heaven and the last judgment. The open-minded Jew is always
deeply impressed by Jesus' opinions, and he understands that
here is one Jew speaking to other Jews."[19]

*   *   *

The Narrow Path, manifestly the best novel about Jesus in Hebrew literature, was written in 1938 by Aharon Abraham Kabak
(1880–1944) and is without a doubt the masterpiece among
his twelve novels.[20] It has been on the list of recommended
books in almost all the secondary schools of Israel for more
than thirty years. Kabak's choice of this theme grew out of an
intense religious experience, which he tries to communicate in
a book full of biblical ecstasy. His Jesus, firmly rooted in his

18. "A New Sensitivity in Judaism and the Christian Message," in *Har-
vard Theological Review*, no. 61 (1968), p. 127.
19. "Inwiefern kann Jesus für Juden eine Frage sein?" in *Concilium*, X,
no. 10 (Oct. 1974), p. 598.
20. English translation by Julian Louis Meltzer, Tel Aviv, 1968.

own Jewish milieu, sacrifices himself body and soul to bring salvation to his people and all of mankind. The narrow, untrod-
den path, Kabak suggests, is that rarest of achievements, the fu-
sion of intense humanity with a divine mandate.

Shortly after the appearance of the first edition, the author
felt impelled to tell his friends how the book had ripened in his
mind: "Several years ago I was seriously sick, bedridden for
months on end. In my heart I had already said good-bye to life
and all my friends and dear ones. What lay in store for me, I
thought, was either a prolonged illness or, if I were lucky, a
speedy end. And then one evening, as I lay by myself, I saw
through the open window the top of a cypress which swayed
gently but incessantly in the wind, all by itself in the open
air. . . . The days of my life passed in review before me, my
stormy youth and my restless years of wandering—and I
thought: In all those storms and troubles there really was
never a time when I wasn't lonely, even with all my friends,
lonely and utterly alone. And now I lay by myself in my
sickbed. I would leave this world alone, as I had once entered
it, lonely and isolated. Then a great terror came over me. Fear
of the appalling darkness which shrouds man's fate on earth
seized me with all its might. At that instant something or
someone whispered in my ear: And what about *him?* . . . The
prisoner in my innards, whose voice I had silenced all my life,
now took advantage of my hour of weakness to leave his cell and
to whisper to me: And what about *him?*

"And our Father in heaven? You came from him, you've
wandered through your life with him, and you're going back to
him. You didn't come into this world alone, and you're not
going to leave it alone either. No! You've never left the bosom
of your Father, even if you didn't realize it. . . . Suddenly, at a
stroke, I knew that I hadn't been alone for a single moment of
my life. And a wellspring of light and joy shot up in my heart.
For the first time since my sickness began I broke into tears. I

cried for joy, for utter happiness. And I promised, if God
should let me recover, I would write a book to tell unhappy
people—as I myself had been—that they were not solitary orphans in the world of the Almighty, nor shifting sand in a deso-
late wasteland. No one who is God's image can be that."[21]

Kabak had been an agnostic all his life, with earthbound
hopes and ambitions, but now he was inspired by a genuine
spiritual awakening. Through Jesus, "that poor, great Jew from
Nazareth," Kabak wanted to describe the human pilgrimage to
the kingdom of heaven on earth. He liberates the Nazarene
from all the fetters of mystical deification and makes him into
a prophet whose teachings are nurtured by the sources of messianic Judaism. Typical of the calm self-confidence with which
he solves even the knottiest dilemmas is the conversation between Jesus and Simon (Peter) on resistance to the Roman
domination: "In those days Jesus often went on long walks. He
bade farewell to the places where he had become accustomed
to praying all by himself. He went to the caves at Arbel. He
was surprised to hear the voices of children ringing out in this
abandoned mountain country, and he came closer. On the far
side of the brook, at the foot of the rock wall, stood a group of
children flocking around a man. . . . It was Simon. They were
all armed with bows and arrows. A sharp sorrow ran through
Jesus, as if one of the arrows had pierced him. He turned
around without a word, to hurry from the spot. The path along
the seashore was deserted, as lonely as his heart. After a long
while he looked back and saw Simon, followed by the children,
who were struggling to catch up with him. . . . Simon left the
children, hurried ahead, and placed himself in the path of
Jesus, who unhesitatingly challenged him:

" 'What are you doing with the little ones, Simon?'

21. *Davar* literary supplement, Tel Aviv, Jan. 13, 1939.

" 'I'm showing them the caves, and I told them what Herod
did to the Jews who sought refuge here.'

" 'Why do you sow hatred in young hearts and turn their
thoughts to bloodshed?'

" 'Hatred only for those who hate Israel!'

" 'What good fruit can hatred bring forth?'

" 'Look around, rabbi,' Simon answered, describing a semicir-
cle with his right hand. 'Behind you lies Tiberias, in front of
you Beth Saida-Julia. Don't these names remind you of our
slavery under the Gentile yoke—the tyranny, the outrages? The
Roman Caesar flaunts his image on every denarius—every coin
carries his godless name. The Idumean is a Roman slave, and
we are the slaves of that slave. You live in yourself, rabbi, and
you don't understand the evil cunning of the world. From
childhood on we've been taught that our land cannot be sold
for all eternity, but we and our land have been sold to the
violators of our people. . . . Day by day that idolator sends
deeper roots down into our earth. From Jerusalem to Caesarea,
from Tiberias to Akko, they befoul the land with theaters, cir-
cuses, and their damned images, to drive us out everywhere.
Should we become strangers in the homeland of our fathers? . . . Those are the things I'm implanting in the hearts
of our children. For our many sins we've been barred from
defending the borders of our country. May they do it, as soon
as they grow up!'

"Jesus was silent awhile, before he turned around to Simon.
He laid his hands on his shoulders and shook him gently, till
Simon looked him straight in the eye. Then he said, 'Son of
man! Listen to me, and don't be afraid of looking inside yourself. . . . Don't let your eyes wander outside, but look into your
heart. . . . An entire world lies inside you, waiting for you.
Within yourself you'll find the spirit of God. . . . Everything
that streams around you out there lives on inside you in just
the same way. That flock of migrating birds flies through your

soul as well; this brook rushes through you too, and the sun shines no less brightly within you. Truly, I say to you, when you discover all this world in yourself, there will be no room left for envy or hatred, for cares about frontiers and land. . . . Simon, wake up!' Again he shook him affectionately by the shoulders and sank his burning glance into the eyes of his friend. . . ."

Here is Kabak's Jesus, speaking with his friend Nakdimon (Nicodemus) a few hours before his crucifixion: "Jesus raised his head, and Nakdimon was once more struck by how much he had aged. But a unique kind of grandeur surrounded him, as though he had already returned from the spirit world. Jesus laid a cool white hand on his companion's black sleeve. 'My teachings,' he said, 'prove there is no need to lament the passing of the kingdom of Rome or Judea. Like the Pharisees, I myself have no need of any earthly kingdom. The kingdom of heaven is enough for me. And like all Sadducees'—here a pale smile trembled on his lips—'I don't believe in a world to come, because I don't believe in death.'

"And then, with a powerful voice, 'Nakdimon, my brother! There is no death in the world. There is only a passing over from one life to another. When all men in all lands no longer believe in death and anchor their faith in a living God, who rules in them and outside them, on the cross there and in the crucified—but in the crucifiers too, then Nakdimon, ah then . . .'" And thus the novel ends with an unfinished sentence, a row of dots—and a living hope.

*　　*　　*

This brief, subjective selection of works about Jesus in Hebrew literature makes no claims to completeness. It is a sampling, not an exhaustive anthology. The 187 Hebrew books, research articles, poems, plays, monographs, dissertations, and essays that have been written about Jesus in the last twenty-seven

years since the foundation of the state of Israel,[22] justify press
reports of a "Jesus wave" in the present-day literature of the
Jewish state. The fact is that much more has been written
about Jesus in Hebrew in the last quarter century than in the
eighteen previous centuries. It took the free intellectual climate
of independence before Jews could deal in such a relaxed fashion with a theme which pressure from the churches had long
ago turned into a Jewish taboo.

"This book was written above all to show that it is possible
to write a life history of Jesus." This beginning of David
Flusser's book *Jesus*[23] expresses the hope of many Israelis
for a credible restoration of the Nazarene, so long given up
for dead, just when scholarly Christian studies of the life of
Jesus seem to have lost faith in such a possibility. "The historical Jesus can no longer be reconstituted from the post-Easter
accounts," Bultmann claimed—whereupon conservative Christian theology withdrew into the impregnable fortress of keryg-
matic Christology.

Could it not be, they ask in Jerusalem, that the rediscovery
of Jesus, thanks to modern biblical sciences, is actually altogether possible, but since the earthly Galilean might turn out
to be thoroughly and uniquely Jewish, it seems better to call off
all search parties as quickly as possible?

Finally, the entire Christology of the churches—and the
same goes for Jewish research on Jesus—is based on secondary
sources, the most reliable of which contains only what Mark
could recall from Peter's memories, thirty-eight years after the
events. And even that much was translated from Aramaic or

22. My list is confined to writers whose principal subject is Jesus of
Nazareth. If one wished to include the scientific monographs that treat
Jesus in connection with other trends in Judaism, the number of writings
would exceed five hundred. Also, the works of Israeli citizens not written
in Hebrew have been left out of account.
23. Hamburg: Rowohlt, 1968.

Hebrew into faulty Greek. But since Qumran anything is possible. More scrolls might be found from the original Christian community, or a copy of the first Our Father, or fragments of the Hebrew gospel. In a country where feverish excavation and construction is the order of the day, where archaeology ranks as a national hobby and every second kibbutz has its own museum, such future finds can no longer be written off as wishful thinking. Israel's threefold return—to the land of its fathers, to existence as a nation, and to the mother tongue of the Bible—favors a vivid appreciation of Jesus and the context of his life such as was scarcely possible till now.

In a recent religious dialogue in Jerusalem, a young Israeli poet said, "In the oldest texts of the Gentile Church the word for incarnation is *enanthroposis,* in other words, 'becoming man.' That is precisely our goal. After God's great retreat into darkness we long as never before for a true incarnation of the sons of Adam. A humanization in the sense of breaking out of the prison of one's own skin and breaking through to one's fellow men. In order to break out of the satanic circle of egoism, which objectifies all our contemporaries into a loveless *id,* we have no need either of a Son of God or of a Holy Ghost but of a true human brother who can set an example of an ideally human existence. One who has the courage to answer with a loud Yes to Cain's question, 'Am I my brother's keeper?' Who is ready to give his life for his brothers, so that he can say, even on the cross, 'Of those whom thou gavest me I lost not one.' That is the fifth Jesus, not the one the four evangelists give us but the Jewish Jesus, the one I'm searching for, to give him an exemplary immortality."

The search for this "fifth Jesus," who is no lofty, fleshless figure of light but a Jew with deep roots in the faith of his people, preoccupies these days a growing number of Israeli scholars and authors, whom we can assign to four different categories.

The first and oldest group, to which Klausner, for example, belongs, stresses the non-Jewish elements in Jesus' teaching, the divisive factors which banish Jesus from Judaism. The second group stresses the common ground shared by Jesus and the normative Judaism of his time, and ascribes the un-Jewish as well as anti-Jewish passages in the New Testament to the editorial influence of the later Gentile Church. The third group accentuates his rebelliousness, not only in the uprising, which he at least endorsed, against Rome and Roman ways but also in his resistance to the Sadducean establishment in Jerusalem, whose bourgeois morality and temple ritualism he wanted to replace with an absolute version of the biblical ethos.

The fourth group views the relationship of Jesus to the faith of his people as a creative contrast and harmony, and both its unifying and divisive aspects as growing out of the same native soil. Without detracting from Jesus' positive originality, this school attests, for example, that all the building blocks of the Sermon on the Mount come from rabbinical quarries, while the architecture and style are Jesus' own.

Common to all four groups is the desire to make the basic components of Jesus' teaching relevant to contemporary problems, a more or less conscious pride in the Galilean rabbi who led the West to the God of Israel, and the insight that it is precisely his profound Jewishness which gives him his universality. The deeper the tree's roots have grown into their native earth, the higher its crown towers in the sky and the farther its branches spread.

At a time when the Christ of Christianity seems to be undergoing an identity crisis, for which modern dogmatic theology, hermeneutics, and exegesis propose a series of radically different solutions, it may be significant that in the literature of his homeland Jesus is gaining new substance, relevance, and authenticity.

II

Jesus in Israeli Schoolbooks

"But the Jews lie in everything, they blaspheme in every way our Lord and God Jesus Christ and His Church. . . ." So complained Agobard, bishop of Lyon, around 840 in a letter to his sovereign.[1] Pope Innocent IV in an epistle to King Louis IX dated May 9, 1244, is still more explicit: "The wicked perfidy of the Jews . . . commits such enormities as are stupefying to those who hear of them, and horrible to those who tell them. For, ungrateful to the Lord Jesus Christ . . . they . . . throw away and despise the Law of Moses and the prophets, and follow some tradition of their elders . . . which traditions, are called 'Talmud' in Hebrew. . . . In it are found blasphemies against God and His Christ, and obviously entangled fables about the Blessed Virgin. . . . In traditions of this sort they rear and nurture their children. . . . The above-mentioned abusive books . . . should . . . be burned in fire. . . ."[2]

From this papal command to burn Jewish texts to the burning of Jews themselves was, to be sure, quite a distance. In any

1. *Patrologia Latina* 104, 85–86.
2. Solomon Grayzel, *The Church and the Jews in the XIIIth Century* (New York: Hermon, 1966), pp. 251, 253.

case, the Church's reproach that they taught hatred of Jesus is one of the oldest pretexts for stirring up hatred of Jews. It emerges as early as the second century, with both Melitto, bishop of Sardis and inventor of the "murder of God" legend, and Marcion, the archenemy of the "Jew God."

A brief comparison of the Church Fathers' picture of the Jews with the Tannaitic (Talmud) Fathers' picture of Jesus provides much food for thought. First, however, it must be stressed that the Talmud contains not a single clear-cut reference to the founder of the Church. Jeshua was a common name, and Josephus alone mentions a dozen or so men who bore it. Only the extracanonical Baraita and Tosephta contain a number of allusions which we can attribute with any certainty to the Nazarene. The chief things they mention are Jesus' Pharisaic method of expounding the Scripture, that he left disciples behind, that he was supposed to be stoned to death for "leading the people astray," and that at least one of his disciples could heal the sick in his name.

Later rabbinical polemics were directed not against Jesus but against the Christology of the early Church, whereas the target of patristic attacks was "the Jews"—i.e., the entire people. Thus Origen explains Matthew 27:25: "The blood of Jesus therefore was not only upon the Jews of his age but upon all Jews till the end of the world."[3] In the talmudic treatise Sota 47a, by contrast, we read, "Our masters teach, 'Always let the left hand push away and the right draw on. It should not be as with Elisha who rejected Gehazi with both hands, nor as with Jehoshua, the son of Perachias, who rejected Jesus the Nazarene with both hands.'"

Chrysostom, the "golden mouth," taught, "The synagogue is a whorehouse . . . a hiding place for unclean animals. . . . Never has a Jew prayed to God. . . . They are all possessed by

3. *Exegeticon ad loc.*

the devil."[4] In a baraita to Sanhedrin 43a, on the other hand, it says, "Our wise men teach that Jesus of Nazareth had five disciples: Mattai, Nakkai, Netzer, Buni, and Todah. . . ." Tertullian made the merciless generalization, "The whole synagogue of the sons of Israel killed him [Jesus]," while the Tannaites in Gittin 57a compare Jesus favorably with the pagan prophet Balaam and stress his love for Israel.

Thus the anti-Jewish theology of the Church led to Israel's being damned as "unbelieving" and "godless"—and as early as the year 380 St. Ambrose could praise the incineration of a synagogue as "an act pleasing to God," while one of his rabbinical contemporaries was uttering the cry of global ecumenism: "I call heaven and earth to witness: Whether Jew or non-Jew, man or woman, free or slave—everyone has the divine spark within him according to his deeds."[5] Around the same time Rabbi Abbahu in Caesarea warned about Christian teaching, without intending Jesus or mentioning his name: "If anybody says to you, I am God, he is lying; [if he says,] I am the Son of Man, he will regret it in the end; [if he says,] I will ascend into heaven, he will not do it."[6]

Compared to the brutal name-calling to which the physical brothers of Jesus were so frequently subjected, from the Church Fathers to Martin Luther, these gentle words sound like an excerpt from an ecumenical dialogue of our own day, in which we try to put an end once and for all to the "doctrine of contempt," as Jules Isaac termed the pseudo theology of anti-Semitism. This was the demand of the Second Vatican Council, the World Council of Churches, and numerous church synods in almost all the countries of Christendom. But even today such deceptive clichés as "late Judaism," "avenging God of the Old Testament," and the "Old Testament religion of

4. *Patrologia Graeca* 48, 847–52.
5. *Seder Eliahu Rabba*, ch. X.
6. Sanhedrin 106a.

law" are reprinted every year in new editions of European
schoolbooks. Not only that, but the process of purging Christian religious textbooks of medieval hostility to Jews still remains far behind the proclamations of Rome and Geneva.

Recently a noted religious educator, who freely conceded this
state of affairs, asked me in return, "But has the state of Israel
made a proper review of the image of Jesus in its own schoolbooks?" The blazing flames of Talmud burnings, the age-old
slander of Jews as "Christ-haters" sprang up before my eyes. If
only people then had been able to come up with solid proof for
what is today common knowledge to all Hebraists and Judaists,
how many human lives and cultural treasures might have been
spared!

Still my conversation partner wasn't interested in digging up
the past but in a factual report for the year 1973, at a time
when the modern Jewish state was celebrating its first quarter
century. And in order to answer his question I put together, on
the basis of consultations at the Ministry of Education and the
Hebrew University in Jerusalem, a list of ten representative history books which are in use today in Israeli schools or which
served until recently as required texts.[7]

Since there is no religious instruction per se in the public
schools of Israel, nor do rabbis give Bible classes there—the
only subjects taught are Tanach (Bible—i.e., the Christian "Old

7. No. 1, Jacob Levi, *Yisrael ba'amim* (Tel Aviv: Am Oved, 1946). No.
2, M. Hendel, *Mekorot lelimud ha-historia ha-yisreelit we-ha-klalit* (Tel
Aviv: Chechik, 1953). No. 3, Abramski and Kirschenbaum, *Divre ha-yamim*,
vol. I (Haifa: Yuwal, 1958). No. 4, Michael Hendel, *Yisrael we-ha-amim*
(Tel Aviv: Chechik, 1961). No. 5, Azriel Shochet, *T'kufat ha-bait ha-sheni*
(Tel Aviv: Chechik, 1962). No. 6, Jacob Katz and Moshe Hershko, *Yisrael
we-ha-amim* (Tel Aviv: Dvir, 1962). No. 7, A. Cherikover, *Historia Klalit*
(Romi), (Tel Aviv, 1963). No. 8, U. Rappaport, *Toldot Yisrael bi-tkufat
ha-bait ha-sheni* (Tel Aviv: Amichai, 1967). No. 9, Avivi and Perski, *Toldot
Yisrael* (Tel Aviv: Yawneh, 1970). No. 10, B. Achiya and M. Harpas,
Toldot Am Yisrael (Tel Aviv: Shrebrek, 1971). The reader is further re-
ferred to *Ha-natzrut ha-kduma*, Jerusalem: Ministry of Education, 1971.

Testament"), Talmud, and Jewish history—the theme of Jesus can only come up for discussion in the last of these. To avoid a purely superficial comparison with the "image of Jews" in Christian textbooks, one more point must first be mentioned: We are talking here about schools and teachers with a centuries-old tradition (often because of local laws or fear of church sanctions) which avoided pronouncing the name of Jesus, much less bringing him into the classroom. We are talking about children who know practically nothing about Christianity but who come from homes where personal experience has tempted the parents to look on the cross and the swastika as closely related. One must also consider that we are talking about a theologically autonomous religious community which can teach and explain its view of life and its understanding of God without reference to other creeds.

Of the ten books on which our analysis is based, two are designed for primary schools, the rest for secondary schools. The oldest book was published in 1946; the latest is dated Fall 1971. Quantitatively, the descriptions of Jesus vary from a minimum of barely two lines—although a page and a half in the same text is dedicated to the "messianic ferment"—to a full chapter of over four pages, with Paul getting five pages. Jesus is passed over in silence only in the ultraorthodox schools of the Agudat-Israel, with around 24,000 students, less than 3 per cent of the school population. Seven books called the Nazarene "Yeshu," which is philologically correct and closely corresponds to "Yesu," the ordinary Israeli name for Jesus, but still is an unusual name that singularizes Jesus and puts him on the fringe of Judaism. Only three books call him "Yeshua," which is not only equivalent to the familiar biblical name "Yoshua" but practically identical to "Yehoshua," a common given name in Israel today.

All the texts clearly distinguish between Jesus, whose Jewishness is everywhere emphasized, and the Christology of

the later Church. Seven of the texts also distinguish between
the Nazarene and the first Christian community. No less prom-
inently stressed are contemporary influences on Jesus, his
training in the Torah, and the fundamental biblicity of his
message. Paul is without exception characterized as the founder
of the Church and the cause of its breaking away from Judaism. In this context some of the books make use of the pun
"He transformed a sect [kat] into a religion [dat]." In other re-
spects most of the authors lean heavily on the Jewish interpretation of Jesus, as given in the works of the historians
Heinrich Graetz, Simon Dubnov, and Joseph Klausner. But
now to the texts themselves.

"Among Pilate's crimes his ordering the crucifixion of Jesus
the Nazarene, who lived and was active at that time, is especially notorious." This line and a half (in Hebrew), which
closes the chapter "Pontius Pilate, Tyrant and Oppressor" in
history book No. 9, is an attempt to deal with Jesus as quickly
as possible, though not to his discredit. The context of the passage makes it clear that Jesus stood on the side of the Jewish
freedom fighters and that his crucifixion was an act of the brutal procurator's policy of anti-Jewish oppression.

The following chapter, "Messianic Ferment," does not actually mention Jesus by name but speaks of the "heralds of the
end of time . . . and men who proclaimed themselves Messiahs
and redeemers," whom not only many Jews "but foreigners as
well believed in." The increasing exploitation by the Romans
and their Jewish collaborators, the poverty of the peasantry,
and longing for the promised redemption from the brutal Gentile yoke are listed as the leading causes of the "messianic ferment."

Almost as laconic is the oldest text, from the year 1946 (No.
1), which devotes the following lines to Jesus and his disciples
under the heading "A Messianic Jewish Sect": "Such a messianic sect was the group from which the Christian religion

later emerged. Its adherents believed in a Messiah named Yeshua, who appeared in the land of Israel, was taken prisoner
and crucified by the Romans, but arose again on the third day
after his burial in a tomb hewn in the rock. Afterwards he as-
cended into heaven, to return to the faithful in due time. The
members of this sect, therefore, waited for the return of their
Messiah, and differed only in this longing from the rest of the
people of Israel. . . . Messianic expectation was deeply and
firmly rooted in the hearts of the entire nation at that time. No
wonder there were Jews who thought the Messiah had already
come." There follow roughly two pages on the gradual separation of the early Church from its "mother," a page and a half
on "Saul of Tarsus," two pages on the "Jesus legend," and a
page on "Jewish Christians and Gentile Christians."

Jesus' Origins

Only six of the ten books examine Jesus' birth, family, and up-
bringing, but those that do clearly discriminate between "plausible facts" and the "later cycle of legends." For example,
"Jesus was the son of a carpenter in Nazareth. He studied the
Torah at the feet of a scribe. . . . He probably also read eschatological books and works of edification, so widespread at the
time of the second temple" (No. 5). "Jesus came from Nazareth. . . . His family belonged to the common people" (No.
8). "Yeshu (Yeshua) was the son of Joseph, a carpenter from
Nazareth, and his wife Miriam" (No. 7). Four books subsequently make mention of the virgin birth, the slaughter of the
innocents in Bethlehem, Jesus' descent from David, and his resurrection in connection with the later "cycle of legends." All
four emphasize the Gentile origin of these "myths" and suggest

that they infiltrated the original belief in Jesus in the wake of
Paulinism as an accommodation to Gentile tastes.

John the Baptist

Five of the ten books mention John the Baptist, as either the
spiritual precursor or the teacher of Jesus. All the passages referring to him, which vary from four to sixteen lines, describe him
as an all but heroic figure: "The simple folk in Galilee long-
ingly awaited the redeemer, each according to his own mentality and point of view. Yochanan too was taken for such a
redeemer. Because of his summons to baptism in the Jordan, to
cleanse the soul in view of the coming redemption, he was
called John the Baptist. He was executed by Herod Antipas out
of fear of a revolutionary uprising. . . . Jesus too was certainly
drawn by such movements. . . . His conviction grew that the
same task which his predecessor, Yochanan the Baptist, had
begun now was assigned to him" (No. 4).

"Yochanan, called the Baptist, was a hermit who summoned
the people to repentance. . . . At that time of intense messianic expectation he made a great stir among the multi-
tudes. . . . The Gospels view him as a sort of prophet Elijah
heralding the arrival of Jesus the Messiah" (No. 5).

"At the time of the political and social ferment in the land
of Israel which preceded the war of the Jews against Rome,
many men who saw themselves as the Messiah arose from
among the people, stirred them up against the Romans, and
prophesied that redemption would be soon in coming. . . .
One of these men was Yochanan. . . . One of his disciples was
Yeshu (Yeshua). . . . He too cured the mentally ill" (No. 7).

". . . in his youth Yeshu belonged to the group of people
who had had themselves baptized by Yochanan. . . . This con-

tact bears witness to the relationship between Jesus and the eschatological currents within Judaism during that epoch. . . . After his baptism at the hands of Yochanan, Yeshu began to preach the coming of the kingdom of God" (No. 8).

The Message of Jesus

Seven of the books mention the gospel of Jesus, which they generally call his teaching (torah). All seven see his announcement of the coming kingdom of heaven as the core of the kerygma, all stress the Judaic nature (i.e., dependence on the Bible) of his preaching. Five quote fairly long excerpts from the New Testament to establish his fidelity to the Torah. Three underscore his ties to the Pharisees, and only one (No. 6) accuses him of anti-Semitism.

Two books point to affinities between the Dead Sea scrolls and the eschatology of Jesus. Here are some typical excerpts: "Jesus preached a morally pure life and the duty to forgive all men, even evildoers and enemies" (No. 3). "Jesus' moral challenges, all of which spring up from the native soil of Jewish ethics, especially in regard to social justice—against the rich and for the poor—made him the hero of the day" (No. 4). "His influence stemmed chiefly from his urgent moral preaching, which met the aspirations of the masses of poor people halfway. In his ethical demands—even if all the sayings ascribed to him are truly his—we find little that is new if we compare his words with those of the scribes of his time" (No. 5). "His disciples greatly revered him and looked on him as a saint. Gradually he too began to believe in himself that he was sent from God. Then he started to express the opinion that one need not keep the laws of the Torah according to the tradition of the wise men but that he had the authority to interpret the Torah

in his own way" (No. 6). "Jesus wandered from city to city in
Galilee and preached in the synagogues about a purer way of
life and coming redemption" (No. 7). "After the baptism by
Yochanan Jesus began to preach the advent of the kingdom of
heaven. . . . Jesus wandered through Galilee with this message
and attracted many people. . . . His sermons concentrated
mainly on ethics. The faith he demanded knew no bounds and
did not require exact compliance with all the prescriptions of the
law. The true believer was above all supposed to be completely
honest, for Jesus especially hated hypocrisy. His relations with
all men were distinguished by brotherliness and love" (No. 8).

Claiming to Be the Messiah

Only one of the books says that Jesus thought "he was the
Messiah" (No. 10). Another (No. 5) is of the opinion that his
later messianic consciousness derives from his disciples. Three
books do not mention the claim at all, while five books state
that only his disciples and supporters, not Jesus himself,
claimed he was the Messiah.

"The members of the [Christian Jewish] sect believed in a
Messiah, whose name was Yeshua" (No. 1). "In the eyes of his
disciples he was a Messiah, who united in himself the qualities
of a man and a Son of God" (No. 3). "In the course of time he
was elevated in the eyes of his followers to a Messiah, a Son of
God" (No. 4). "His disciples began to see in him the Messiah
who would lead them into the kingdom of God—and he too
started to look on himself in this way" (No. 5). "His few disciples from among the country people [am ha-aretz] accompa-
nied him on his wanderings and looked upon him as the Messiah. . . . His appearance in Jerusalem awakened concern in the

heart of the priests who had legitimate reasons to fear 'Messiahs' and false prophets" (No. 7). "Yeshua of Nazareth, who promised to redeem his people, fell, like others before him who had considered themselves the Messiah, into the hands of the Roman authorities. . . . It is hard to ascertain to what degree Yeshua understood himself as the Messiah or the Son of God. . . . It may be that late in his career he did see himself as Messiah, as is possible to infer from his words and deeds in Jerusalem" (No. 8). "Yeshu of Nazareth . . . gathered a great circle of disciples, with whom he went up to Jerusalem, animated by the faith that he was the Messiah and that he could convince the people to recognize him as such" (No. 10).

Conviction and Crucifixion

Seven of the books impute the death of Jesus (two texts call it "the murder of Yeshu") to the Romans and make Pontius Pilate, whose atrocities are documented by history, the major offender. The story of Jesus' passion gains a considerable contemporary flavor from the fact that "procurator" is rendered by the same word in Hebrew (natziv) used to designate the British High Commissioner in Palestine, under whose regime several Jewish freedom fighters were condemned and executed in 1946–47.

Four of the books draw a clear connection between the claim that Jesus was the Messiah—whether made by Jesus himself, his disciples, or the masses—and his politically motivated conviction. Only two books by and large follow the talmudic account[8] that the death sentence, in keeping with the Torah, was passed by the Sanhedrin, to be ratified and carried out by Pi-

8. Baraita Sanhedrin 43a.

late. One book (No. 8) devotes a page and a half to a more
probing analysis of the responsibility for Jesus' death. Its main
conclusions will be cited later on.

"He was arrested and crucified by the Romans" (No. 1).
After discussing Jesus' critical "deviations" from standard Judaism—especially the remark "My kingdom is not of this
world," whereby Jesus "repudiated Israel's outlook on life"—
text No. 4 goes on to say, "This fundamental opposition and
antagonism inevitably had to lead to open conflict. According
to the evangelists the Sanhedrin condemned Jesus to death and
handed him over to the Procurator Pilate for execution. In
keeping with Roman custom Jesus was put to death on the
cross."

"Both the betrayal by Yehuda Ish-Krayoth [Judas Iscariot]
and the report of the Sanhedrin's alleged condemning Jesus to
death and delivering him to Pilate for execution are plainly
fictitious. The Sanhedrin at that time had no jurisdiction whatsoever over capital crimes. The evangelists narrate that Jesus'
trial took place on the feast day, which is perfectly unthinkable. In any case, the fact remains that he was crucified by
order of Pilate" (No. 5).

"After his arrival in Jerusalem the Nazarene [this word is
synonomous in Hebrew with Christian] was apprehended as a
perverter of the people, who wished to lead Israel away from
the Torah. He was put on trial by the Sanhedrin and found
guilty. The Sanhedrin delivered him to the Roman governor
named Pontius Pilate. Pilate confirmed Jesus' death sentence,
since he saw in him a rebel against the government who was
seeking to have himself crowned king of the enslaved people of
Israel. The sentence was carried out, and Yeshu was crucified
to a tree [or wood], as the Romans customarily dealt with condemned prisoners" (No. 6).

Compare this with the account from the Baraita Sanhedrin
43a: "On the evening before the Passover feast they hanged

Jesus. Before this, however, a herald had walked before him for forty days, crying out, 'This man is going to be stoned, because he has practiced magic and perverted and divided Israel. Let every man who knows anything in his favor come and plead his case for him.' But they found nothing in his favor and hanged him on the eve of the Passover." According to contemporary talmudic scholarship this legendary baraita dates from the years 180–200, when the Gentile Christian doctrine of the Trinity, in its popular version at any rate, must have struck many rabbis as polytheistic. At that time a number of Jews had "seduced" their brothers into accepting the (Ebionite) faith in Jesus—a crime which, if it involved "other gods," had to be avenged by stoning to death and hanging the corpse, in accordance with Jewish law (Deut 13:7–12). And so the rabbis, with the benefit of hindsight, branded the master and Messiah of these men as a "perverter of the people" and posthumously punished him as such. On these polemically plausible grounds they took full "blame" upon themselves (but they considered their action meritorious) for Jesus' execution, for which they were re- proached—wrongfully, in the light of history—by the Chris- tians.

If the many sayings of Jesus recorded in the Gospels which express his devotion to the Torah have even a grain of histori- cal truth in them, then the charge of "perverting the people" is just as unthinkable as that of "blasphemy" (Mk 14:64; Mt 26:65), which none of the four Gospels show him committing. For neither his claim to be the Messiah (Mk 14:61 ff.), nor the usurpation of "divine sonship" (Mt 26:63 ff.) are considered blasphemy or capital offences in Jewish law.

The above version of the facts, from text No. 6, hopes to find the truth "in medio," and blends elements of the talmudic ac- count with the Gospels to reconstruct the story in a way that is historically not impossible, even if hardly probable. But let us look at the other texts:

"[Jesus'] appearance in Jerusalem awakened concern in the heart of the priests, who were afraid of 'would-be Messiahs' and false prophets. No less concerned was the Roman procurator, for any disturbance among the people could easily lead to an anti-Roman revolutionary movement. Hence Pilate ordered Jesus to be taken into custody and brought before his tribunal. His verdict was crucifixion" (No. 7).

"The Roman authorities, who suspected everyone, saw in Yeshu a political rebel threatening the security of their regime. The Roman governor, therefore, commanded him to be crucified as a rebel against the state" (No. 10).

The following are excerpts from text No. 8, which devotes considerable space to a discussion of the passion story: "Jesus' activity in Jerusalem . . . brought about his arrest and execution. . . . His death on the cross is the cornerstone of anti-Semitism in Christian countries, which rests on the charge that the Jews are 'murderers of the Messiah.' . . . After Jesus had stirred up the feelings of the people . . . the servants of the high priest took him into custody and brought him before the Sanhedrin, which found itself in a delicate situation. . . . Even a peace-loving 'Messiah' could have jeopardized public order then . . . particularly at Passover time, when many thousands of pilgrims crowded the Holy City and disturbances had often broken out before. . . . Jesus' arrest ensued, most likely for security reasons. Nevertheless, according to the Gospels the charges brought against him were predominantly religious in nature. . . . On the following day Jesus was brought before the Roman governor, who condemned him to be crucified, ostensibly as a claimant to the title 'King of the Jews,' which certainly alludes to Jesus as the Messiah but points as well to his rebellion against Roman authority. The idea of the Messiah in itself represented a clear rejection of that authority and was considered seditious. . . . The arrest of Jesus was handled by the high priests, but the governor pronounced sentence. . . . The story that the Jews forced Pilate to crucify Jesus derives from Christian theology. . . . At that time only Pilate had authority to impose the death penalty. . . . Crucifixion as a form of capital punishment is unknown to Jewish law. . . . Jesus was not the only 'Messiah' whom the Romans murdered. . . . In any case, the crucifixion of Jesus became the central event of Christianity" (No. 8). On this score it must be explained that expressions like "for security reasons," "he died for many," "taken into custody," and "execution" sound only too familiar to Israeli ears—and help to bring Jesus into the realm of personal experience or of recent history.

The Gospels

Six of the books quote a total of eighteen New Testament passages, covering Jesus' birth, baptism, preaching, and passion. The most quoted section is the Sermon on the Mount, followed by Matthew 10:5 ff. ("Go nowhere among the Gentiles . . ."), Matthew 15:21–28 (the Syro-Phoenician woman), Matthew 22:34–40 (the question concerning the first commandment), and Acts 1:6 ff. (Restoration of the kingdom of Israel). All the quotations come from the Delitzsch translation of the New Testament, which is easily obtainable in Israel, without cost, from the various Christian missionary organizations. Three books give detailed explanations of the historical, literary, and religious meaning of the four Gospels, their various biases, and the similarities and differences of the first three (the so-called Synoptic problem).

In two books quotations from the Old Testament are juxtaposed with quotations from the New so as to point out similarities and affinities. None of the books mentions the divergencies between the Gospels in particulars, nor is the medieval libel

Toledot Yeshu (also known as the antigospel) either mentioned or cited.

Early Christianity in the Official Curriculum

In hopes of finding a common denominator for all these different treatments of Jesus and Christianity in the schools, in 1971 the Israeli Ministry of Education published a curriculum with matching texts, bearing the title *Ha-natzrut ha-k'duma* (Early Christianity). The text designed for the pupils in their seventh year of school, that is for twelve- and thirteen-year-olds, was compiled by a group of educators in consultation with a number of university professors and distributed for experimental use as part of the program of readings for history classes. A revised and improved edition of this text is currently in preparation.

The thirty-five-page volume contains seventeen illustrations, including a fresco of the crucifixion from the Church of Santa Maria Antiqua in Rome, catacombs, Christian symbols from the early Church, some cathedrals and church buildings, an altar, a baptismal font, and an anonymous depiction of the Last Supper from the sixth century. The text also contains eight extensive excerpts from the New Testament, as well as the text of the Nicene Creed. The four chapters of the volume are entitled:

1. Jesus and the First Christians (eight pages),
2. Christianity Becomes the Religion of the Roman Empire (twelve pages),
3. The Christian Religion and the Church (ten pages),
4. The Church and the Jews (five pages).

Since this is the first official school text in Israel which tries to do justice to Jesus in ecumenical fashion—so far as this is consistent with the basic principles of Judaism—let us translate verbatim a number of key passages:

"To what extent was the activity of Yeshu affected by the position of the people [Israel] at that time?" This is the opening question on the first page, to which the rest of the chapter attempts to work out an answer. The following introduction suggests the general drift of the presentation: "The epoch after the death of Herod was a hard time for the Jewish people. The Roman governors, who ruled Israel with an iron hand, stirred up popular resistance to their regime. There were Jews, such as the Essenes, who withdrew into the desert in order to live far apart from the great centers of population. Others bowed their heads and waited for the fury to pass, while a third group founded communities of zealots who were firmly resolved to overthrow the Roman yoke by force. In addition to this, one Messiah after another arose from among the people. These men saw themselves as divine emissaries and gathered throngs of people about them, to whom they promised to bring redemption. Such messianic movements were ruthlessly suppressed by the Romans." A section on "Yeshu" links up with this fourfold reaction to the Pax Romana.

"This was the reality in the world where Jesus was born. We do not know much about his life and very little about his childhood. The four narratives in the 'Gospels' in the 'New Testament' are the only source we have. [A footnote explains 'Gospels.'] According to these accounts Yeshu was born to the carpenter Joseph and his wife Miriam from Nazareth. Joseph's house was a true Jewish home, faithful to the Law. Here Yeshu grew up and absorbed God's Torah. . . . Like many Jews of those days Joseph's family was accustomed to make a yearly pilgrimage to Jerusalem to celebrate the feast of Passover. It is easy to imagine the impression that Jerusalem and

the Temple—then at the very peak of their glory—must have
made on the soul of the Galilean boy. . . . At the age of thirty
Yeshu's life came to a turning point when he met Yochanan
the Baptist. This Yochanan baptized in the vicinity of Jericho,
publicly proclaimed that the kingdom of heaven was coming
soon, and summoned the Jews to prepare themselves in haste
for this event: to repent and make amends, to purify their
souls, and to plunge into the Jordan to cleanse their bodies."
After two quotations, from Josephus and Matthew,[9] there follows a paragraph entitled "Jesus Preaches in Galilee":

"After he was baptized, Yeshu did not return home but
began to wander through the villages and cities of Galilee. He
preached to the people everywhere, now in the synagogue and
another time in the mountains; once he even spoke in a boat
on the Lake of Kinnereth. Many people came to hear him, and
some were so moved by him that they left their homes and
families to join with Yeshu and follow him wherever he went.
Who were those people who followed Yeshu—and what had
won their hearts?"

As a help in answering these two key questions, the text
quotes long excerpts from the Sermon on the Mount, and suggests to the teacher the following three questions for written
homework assignments:

1. Who were the men to whom Yeshu addressed himself?
2. Which promises of Yeshu moved the hearts of his listeners?
3. What did Yeshu demand of his disciples, to enable
   them to reach the promised goal?

The text explains the concept of the kingdom of heaven, and
then continues, "Aside from his sermons Yeshu, according to
the Gospels, also did things which impressed the people as miracles. In one village he cured cripples, and elsewhere—it is told

9. Josephus, *Antiquities* XVIII, 116–17; Mt 3:1–2, 4–6, 13.

—he fed a great multitude with a few loaves and fishes which
he had with him. Yeshu became famous and, as his success
grew, his disciples—and Yeshu himself—began to look upon
him as the Messiah, who would bring redemption and the kingdom of heaven. The words and deeds of Yeshu stirred up a
good deal of resistance, both among the country people and,
much more, among the ruling elite. When Yeshu saw that the
authorities intended to kill him, he decided to leave Galilee
and to go up to Jerusalem."

While in the previous section the word "authorities" has an
ambiguous ring to it, the following lines from a section entitled
"Yeshu in Jerusalem" clarify the situation: "On the days before
the feast of Passover the streets of Jerusalem resounded with
the cries of swarms of pilgrims who had come to celebrate the
feast. The throng was especially great in the forecourts of the
Temple, the goal of all pilgrims. Yeshu too headed for the
Temple as soon as he arrived in Jerusalem. But what he saw
there made him very angry. He saw before him a crowd of
buyers and sellers, the tables and stalls of the shopkeepers set
up everywhere to satisfy the needs of the visitors. Yeshu became furious, seeing in all that a desecration of the Temple. In
a fit of rage he assaulted the shopkeepers and overturned their
tables—charging them with turning the house of God into a
den of thieves. In the forecourt of the sanctuary Yeshu repeated his message and called upon the crowd to do penance
and prepare themselves for the kingdom of heaven. He
addressed the priests in the Temple as well and accused them
of profaning it. His harsh words ended with the prophecy that
it would not be long before the sanctuary was completely destroyed."

The final section likewise follows the Synoptic tradition for
the most part, but takes the latest research into consideration
in treating the trial of Jesus. For the founding of the Eucharist
the text follows Matthew, translating "my body," in keeping

with the style of the Hebrew Bible, back into Hebrew as "my
flesh." The word "blood" occurs twice, and is likewise rendered
in a way that faithfully reflects the rhythms of Hebrew speech.
Under the heading "The Last Supper" we read, "Some days
after the events in the Temple Yeshu and his disciples gathered
to celebrate the Passover in one of the houses in Jerusalem. But
hearts were heavy at their festive table. Yeshu knew that his
words and deeds in the Temple would have repercussions. The
authorities could not ignore a man who insisted he was the
Messiah, who disturbed the peace and warned that the Temple
would be destroyed. His disciples too were afraid the end was
near. Yeshu gave voice to these feelings when he broke bread.
He divided it among his disciples and said, 'Take and eat, for
this is my flesh.' After he had spoken the blessing over the cup
of wine, he said, 'Drink of this, all of you, for this is my blood,
the blood of the new covenant, which is shed for many for the
forgiveness of sins.' A short time after the meal Yeshu was
placed under arrest by messengers of the high priests and
brought up for interrogation."

In its account of the hearing before the Sanhedrin the school
text goes beyond the descriptions of the three Synoptics. "At
the interrogation Yeshu declared he was the Messiah, the Son
of God. When the high priest heard this, he tore his garments
and ordered Yeshu to be taken before the tribunal of the
Roman governor, Pilate." In the final paragraph, entitled "The
Crucifixion of Yeshu," it must be emphasized that the equivo-
cal phrase "You have said so" sounds in Hebrew like a clear
"Yes": "To Pilate's question, 'Are you the king of the Jews?'
Yeshu answered, 'You say it,' and for that he was sentenced to
death on the cross as a rebel against the Empire. But the matter was not at an end. Three days after his death—so said his
disciples—he arose from the dead, appeared to his disciples, and
announced to them that he would soon return and the kingdom of heaven would then become a reality. Accepting the tes-

timony of these disciples, a group of the faithful gathered together to wait for his return."

The first chapter concludes with two appendices, the text of
the passion according to Mark and a picture of an Italian pietà,
followed by three suggestions for homework exercises:

1. What were the main ideas which Jesus expressed?
2. Who followed him, and who opposed him?
3. Why was Jesus executed?

The next three sections of the manual discuss the history of the
development of Christianity from the first community to the
"victory" under the emperor Constantine. After that ten pages
are devoted to church dogma, the sacraments, and the "basic
principles of the Christian faith." The last chapter, "The
Church and the Jews," attempts to explain the phenomenon of
the Church's hatred of Jews as objectively as possible, *sine ira
et studio*. One of the topics assigned for homework suggests the
authors' point of view: "The Christians considered themselves
the true Israel. Did this help to promote a feeling of community between Christians and Jews—or did the opposite take
place?" But we shall go into that later on.

A year after the publication of the first edition of the syllabus on "Early Christianity," the Ministry of Education distributed a manual designed to help teachers implement the
religious education curriculum, which, it is frequently stressed,
aims at opening up new instructional territory. The origins of
Christianity and church history have been receiving serious attention at the Hebrew University in Jerusalem for more than a
decade now, while most secondary schools and universities have
been studying the history of early Christianity since the middle
fifties. To be sure, the amount of class time devoted to these
subjects, the particular emphases, and the degree of objectivity
and scholarly accuracy attained have all varied, depending on
the teaching personnel available at any given time. The main

purpose of both official publications is to do justice pedagogi-
cally to this topic and in so doing to dissipate the emotions
aroused by this extremely sensitive chapter in Jewish history.

Thus the foreword to the teachers' manual states, "The position which Christianity and the Church occupy in the history
of world civilization requires no special emphasis. Their
influence has been so pervasive that we can scarcely imagine
trying to understand that civilization without some prior
knowledge, even if superficial, of Christianity. This chapter ac-
quires a peculiar importance from the fact that we are Jews.
Christianity's attitude towards Judaism has had a deep and
tragic influence on the fate of the Jewish people for two thousand years. We have endeavored to discuss the history of early
Christianity as matter-of-factly as possible, without making any
value judgments. It seems important to us that the teacher
know the difference between a factual explanation and a subjective evaluation. . . ."

On page 2 the subject is divided into the four topics:

1. Jesus and the First Christians,
2. Christianity Becomes the Religion of the Empire,
3. Christianity and the Church,
4. The Church and the Jews.

After a list of recommended readings (around a page long) for
teachers who wish to broaden their knowledge in this area,
there follows a second list, of key concepts (e.g., the Messiah,
the kingdom of heaven, baptism, the Gospels) to be defined
and discussed in class in connection with the first theme. Four
central aspects of Jesus' career receive special attention here:

1. Jesus the Nazarene as a Jew (focus on the Jewish elements in his life!),
2. Jesus as a rebel against Judaism (ideologically and practically),
3. Jesus in the eyes of the Jewish leaders of his time,

4. The principal ideas of Jesus:
   a) the content of his preaching (the values he wished to see realized),
   b) the foundation he gave his teaching (concentrate on his indebtedness to the Bible).

Under the heading "Suggested Procedures" we find the piece of advice which recently led to an indignant lead article in the Orthodox press as well as some cries of protest in Parliament: "Similarities and contrasts between Jesus and one of the prophets of Israel—for example, Elijah—should be developed. One of the students could be directed to prepare a list explaining what Elijah and Jesus had in common and where they differed. It is assumed that students will see the closest similarities in their ethical preaching and the miracles which both of them worked. With respect to the contrasts, the fact should be pointed out that Jesus does not claim to be a prophet, yet he dares to say things which no prophet before him had ever expressed (thus, for instance, in the Sermon on the Mount, where he contradicts the statutes of the Torah: 'But I say to you . . .')."

The lead article in *Hamodia*, the daily newspaper of the rather small Orthodox party Agudat-Israel (four seats in Parliament, out of 120) spoke out on January 26, 1973: "Christian proselytizers could not have celebrated a more glorious victory than the one which the following situation (recently discovered by mere accident) has helped them to. Their work, it seems, is being done for them by Jewish teachers working for the government—and no one raises any objections. On the contrary! People try to hush up the bitter outcry which has arisen to protest against . . . Christian preaching in Israeli schools . . . against the introduction of Christian elements into Jewish education. . . . Nowadays Jewish students are asked to draw comparisons between the prophet Elijah and 'that man' [the usual phrase for Jesus in the Jewish Middle Ages]!"

This article presents the facts with complete accuracy, as the president of the Knesset had to admit when the deputies of the Agudat-Israel party later tried to put an immediate debate about this "public scandal" on the agenda. But since it was a question of a duly authorized part of the new secondary-school curriculum (which devotes no less time, effort, and tolerance to Islam) already in use for the past three years, the presidium of the Knesset saw no pressing need to recognize this request, and referred it instead to the parliamentary committee on education.

At least one hour of instruction is to be given over to the Sermon on the Mount, to explain the ethical stance of the Nazarene. This class is supposed to present extensive excerpts from the Hebrew text of the New Testament and a series of rabbinical parallels. In addition the theme of "Jesus as a Jew" is to be thoroughly discussed in an open forum in the classroom. In the course of this, four different standpoints are to get a hearing: Jesus' own sense of himself, and the attitudes towards him of the high priest, of Pontius Pilate, and finally of the apostles. To foster a sympathetic understanding of the problem, teachers are requested to stage the trial of Jesus in the classroom, with students taking on the roles of accusers as well as defenders of Jesus. The apostles should speak in his defense, and accuse the Roman authorities of executing an innocent Jew.

The second theme, "Christianity Becomes the Religion of the Empire," raises five important questions:

1. Why did a Jewish sect develop into an independent religion?
2. What alterations and innovations did Paul make in Jesus' teaching?
3. What circumstances promoted the success of Christianity?

4. What influence did the Roman persecutions have on early Christianity?
5. What motivated emperor Constantine to legalize the new religion?

Teachers are asked to stress the fact that "Jesus himself founded no community, and only after his death did one come into being through his disciples, in expectation of his return."

The next paragraph, entitled "Motives," poses two questions for thorough debate by the class:

1. Paul decided that a Christian need not live according to the prescriptions of the Torah. Would Yeshu have agreed with him?
2. How did it happen that a peripheral little Jewish sect became a worldwide religion with almost a billion members?

To bring the subject to life, students are shown photographs of catacombs, Christian symbols, medieval cathedrals, and Renaissance paintings, along with maps illustrating the gradual spread of Christianity. Teachers point out that this growth "originated in areas settled by Jews."

In treating the persecutions as a factor in the emergence of the early Church—a subject with many parallels in Jewish history—teachers are urged to give prominence to the notion that "the bravery of Christian martyrs increased the prestige of their faith and convinced many people of its truthfulness."

Finally, a lengthy paragraph attempts to restore the objective sense of a concept which for Jews is charged with dark memories from the past. "The term 'mission' has two meanings: One is practical—the propagation of the faith; the other is psychological—the personal desire to spread one's beliefs, even in the face of death."

The third theme, "Christianity and the Church," deals chiefly with basic theological concepts, most of which have no exact parallels either in Judaism or the Hebrew language—e.g., justification, the Trinity, sacrament, mass, communion, original sin. These ideas must first be explained and then translated.

At this point a group of five questions is offered for classroom discussion. All students are encouraged to voice their opinions freely on the following:

1. The effects of the institutionalization of the Church on the life and thought of the faithful;
2. The Church as an association—its structure, authority, and its place in the life of Christians;
3. Relations between Church and State—problems of double allegiance;
4. The representation of God in Christianity—the person of Jesus, oneness of the Trinity;
5. The historical basis of Christianity—historical events which later took on mystical significance.

Since this chapter will most likely make the greatest demands on the student, it is up to each teacher whether he wishes to pursue some of these abstract issues still further or skip over them. Should he decide, however, to do this introduction to Christian theology—remember, we are talking about school children from twelve to thirteen years of age—he must make two notions extremely clear: "A. The Church's dogma of the two natures of Jesus, the divine and the human. B. The question of monotheism—the principle of unity within the Trinity."

In the face of the explosiveness and complexity of these questions—the subject of innumerable medieval disputations—all teachers are given a warning: "In debating these issues in school it is important to refrain from even faint criticism, which might occasion a contemptuous attitude on the part of the students. . . . One had best limit oneself to a factual presentation of the Christian faith and avoid all value judgments."

Under the rubric "Methodology" the authors recommend

visits to the city museum and studying illustrated volumes on church art, along with the additional suggestion that "a visit to a church might be scheduled as part of the annual class outing, to help the students to visualize better the Christian atmosphere and the liturgy of the Church."

The fourth and last chapter, "The Church and the Jews," could easily provoke strong emotional reactions, and so teachers are warned to weigh every word here and to outline the situation "as objectively as possible." Students and teachers together are now to analyze and try to shed some light on four questions:

1. The attitude of Christians to the Bible,
2. Biblical figures in Christian perspective,
3. What is "Israel according to the flesh" and "Israel according to the spirit" (or "the true Israel")?
4. The ambivalent Christian view of the Jews.

To encourage objectivity, teachers are counseled to have their students ask themselves the question, "How do the Jewish people appear from a Christian point of view?" To help answer it, a sort of theological balance sheet is proposed, which summarily lists Jewish "debit" and "credit" in parallel columns:

The Jewish People from a Christian Point of View

Credit:	Debit:
chosen by God	stubborn and rebellious
received the commandments on Sinai	transgressed God's laws
served God	persecuted the prophets
preserved the Bible and passed it on	killed Jesus
the prophets arose from its midst	rejected Jesus' teaching
brought forth Jesus	

The manual ends with some practical advice of a biblical stamp, directed both to teachers and students in the spirit of fairness: "Let us try to think ourselves into the position of a

Christian who has just drawn up this balance sheet of the Jewish people. What is his attitude to Jews likely to be?"

The reactions from faculty members to the new manual have been "amazingly positive," as a senior official of the Ministry of Education ascertained not long ago. The vast majority advocates this pedagogical trend towards tolerance and openness from personal conviction, and believes that it has a place in the religious sphere as well. Only a small minority, made up almost exclusively of teachers who characterize themselves as nonreligious, finds that the image of Jesus and the Church have turned out "all too favorable."

Thanks to a number of constructive suggestions, the authors hope to be able to bring out in the near future a second, corrected edition of the manual and the texts on early Christianity.

In the 1971–72 school year a questionnaire was distributed in various schools to test Israeli children for whatever prior knowledge or prejudices they might have about Christianity before beginning to study it. Several hundred schoolchildren of the most varied social and cultural backgrounds were asked to complete the following sentences while in class:

1. Jesus was . . .
2. He lived around . . . in . . .
3. What he did was . . .
4. Jesus was executed by . . .
5. He died because . . .
6. Today all Christians have . . . in common.
7. A missionary is a man who . . .
8. A bishop is a man who . . .
9. The New Testament is . . .
10. Christianity was founded . . . years ago.
11. Relations between Jews and Christians are . . .

Two sheets of paper were attached to the questionnaire. They were divided into five rectangular boxes, in which each pupil had to enter, "as quickly as possible," his opinion on Arabs, Moses, Christianity, Jesus, and Judaism. The scale of qualities to be checked off went from "nice, true, clean, important, good, strong," to "ugly, bad, weak, useless, dirty."

Although the results of the "population study" were not made public, educators involved in administering it have testified that knowledge of Christianity proved to be rather limited, while emotional attitudes towards Jesus and Christianity were generally positive. Thus, for example, children from Mideastern homes had a uniformly worse opinion of Arabs than children of European origin had of Jesus and Christianity. While only a few were able to date the beginning of Christianity, most looked upon Jesus as a Jew who chose to be baptized—which "betrayal" led to his execution "by the Jews." For about 5 per cent of those questioned this was the reason why "the Christians hate us." Only about one out of thirty children knew what the New Testament was—"the Bible of the goyim" was the usual answer, while a missionary was a man "who preached," and a bishop a man "who worshiped God." None of those questioned (quite different from their parents in this) mentioned any connection between Hitler's genocide, Christianity, and anti-Semitism. Almost 10 per cent, on the other hand, asserted that Christianity as well as Islam had "copied" its faith from Judaism. While the educators found in this answer a nascent chauvinism which they hope to correct with the help of the revised curriculum, the gratifying lack of any association between Christianity and Nazism may be traceable in part to a little booklet by school inspector Dr. Arie L. Bauminger which was introduced in 1967 in all classes beyond the primary level and has been in continual use since then as a teaching aid. It is entitled *Honor Roll*, and it recounts in sixty pages the glorious deeds of some of the "just men of the nations" who risked their lives—many in fact were killed—to rescue Jews during World War II. The fact that these roughly eight hundred "heroes of

charity" came from twenty-three different countries and that
Christian clergymen of all denominations made up a significant
portion of them may well have prevented the trauma of Auschwitz from degenerating into an anti-Christian complex.

* * *

Student questions in classes on Jesus deal in general with three
topics: "What is actually the difference between the message
of John the Baptist and the preaching of Jesus?" "Does Jesus
belong to us now—or to the Christians?" "Why didn't his apostles defend him?" This last question in particular stirred up
strong indignation in all the classes over the "cowardice of the
apostles," who left their rabbi in the lurch just when his life
was in danger. There is general resistance to the Christian alle-
gory which sees in the sacrifice of Isaac a prefiguration of the
crucifixion of Jesus. "But Isaac *wasn't* sacrificed," they shout,
"while Jesus died a horrible death!"

The expression "Jewish Christians" at first provokes resound-
ing laughter, since to Israeli ears it sounds something like "poor
millionaires." Only later, when most of the students realize
that, as one of them put it, all of Christianity was actually "a
Jewish invention," does the amusement give way to a more or
less outspoken pride. In reply to the question "What does Israel have to be proud of?" (from a civics examination), a thir-
teen-year-old wrote, "That our Judaism has laid the foundation
for two of the greatest world religions, Christianity and Islam."

Since the sacraments and their efficacy present major difficulties for the youthful understanding of Israeli students, several
teachers in Jerusalem decided to take their charges on a half-
day's outing in the Old City to study the question. Initial anx-
ieties on the part of some parents and girl students were dispelled by contacting Hebrew-speaking nuns, who arranged to
welcome the classes at the first station of the Via Dolorosa.

The nuns clarified such unfamiliar terms as apse, missal, incense, baptismal font, and crucifix by showing them to the children. A couple of pupils could not conceal their disappointment over the absence of catacombs—a word which evidently has a special fascination for young Israelis.

In one of the churches a lively debate flared up over a loaf of bread which one of the students discovered in a mural of the Last Supper. After a long give-and-take the Franciscan father in charge of this part of the tour had to concede that the eighteenth-century painter obviously had not known enough about Judaism to portray Jesus and his disciples at Passover time with matzos.

The only class unable to complete their itinerary was the one from a secondary school which had decided to take on the entire length of the Via Dolorosa. Fourteen stations of uninterrupted agony and torment, often described in full detail by a well-meaning Dominican priest, were more than the youngsters could bear. When the group arrived at the gate of the Church of the Holy Sepulcher, where the final stations are, there were only three students left, and they took to their heels, under the pretext of "terrible headaches."

The general mood on the day after the "Christian trip" was a mixture of joyful surprise at the hearty welcome they had gotten in all the churches and cloisters, and distinct doubts about the many "miracles" which had been served up to them. They came to such conclusions as "I guess there are good and bad Christians, stupid ones and smart ones, the same as with us."

One secondary-school class, which got to observe a group of European pilgrims in the cloister of a Roman Catholic order, the Sisters of Zion, was deeply impressed by the visible devotion of all its members. When one of the nuns, her eyes filled with tears, kissed the stones of the Ecce Homo arch, the students fell silent for a long, thoughtful pause. "Well," said one boy after a while, "our rabbis also kiss the Wailing Wall—and some of them even cry when they do it."

The examination question which most often evokes an emotional response is, "What role did the Jews play in the execution of Jesus?" Students answer by calling the Gospel account of the trial before the Sanhedrin "false" or "pure fiction," although some of them are ready to grant that the Temple party of the Sadducees may have wanted to make common cause with the Romans. Practically all the students mention the fact that Pilate pronounced the death sentence, that crucifixion was a Roman mode of punishment, and that Roman legionaries nailed Jesus to the cross as unassailable proofs of Roman responsibility for Jesus' death. On the whole, students look on Christianity as a kind of Jewish heresy rather than as an entirely new or different religion. And, as many of them pointed out in their questionnaires, they consider Saul of Tarsus to be its founder rather than Jesus.

For most of the students the Nazarene is a sympathetic Jewish idealist, like so many others who were brutally murdered by the Greeks and Romans. His nonconformism seems, in fact, to make him more attractive to many schoolboy rebels—except for his advice to turn the other cheek, which regularly provokes shrugs or laughter.

The current syllabus on early Christianity certainly stands in need of a number of corrections, educators in Jerusalem agree. Still they think they are moving in the right direction to promote, in a positive and practical way, future ecumenical understanding based on the Bible. And this, they feel, must begin in the schools.

In conclusion, we may briefly summarize the leading features of the image of Jesus as found in Israeli schoolbooks:

1. Nowhere is Jesus saddled with responsibility for Christian hatred of the Jews, nor are any negative inferences drawn from the Church to the Nazarene.

2. The Jewishness of Jesus, which is taken for granted in all the texts, does give rise to differing interpretations of his historical role—aspirant Messiah, eschatological herald, seducer of the people, moral preacher, or patriotic rebel against the Gentile yoke. But the end result is an unambiguous, more or less emphatic, sympathy for the Nazarene when it comes to his martyr's death on the Roman cross.

3. Although some texts speak of Jesus' "deviations" from the standard Judaism of his day, they are far outweighed by references to his "fidelity to the Torah," dependence on the Bible, and Jewish ethos.

If we compare this broad outline to the image of Jews in the schoolbooks of the Christian West after Auschwitz, as seen in the critical studies of Theodor Filthaut, Hans Jochen Gamm, Herbert Jochum, Paul Demann, the University of Louvain, Bernard E. Olson, and Charles Y. Glock, it is hard to avoid a feeling of sadness.[10]

With the sole exception of the Gospels—or of their sources—which have been rightly termed documents of Jewish belief, the present day schoolbooks of Israel contain what is undoubtedly the most sympathetic picture of Jesus ever offered to a generation of Jewish children by their teachers. This fact is confirmed by, among other things, the protests of a group of rabbis (most are recent immigrants from America and England) who re-

10. Paul Demann, *La catéchèse chrétienne et le peuple de la Bible* (Paris, 1953). Theodor Filthaut, *Israel in der christlichen Unterweisung* (Munich: Kösel, 1963). Hans Jochen Gamm, *Pädagogische Studien zum Problem der Judenfeindschaft* (Wiesbaden: Luchterhand, 1965). Bernard E. Olson, *Faith and Prejudice* (New Haven: Yale University Press, 1963). Charles Y. Glock and Rodney Stark, *Christian Beliefs and Anti-Semitism* (New York: Harper & Row, 1966). *Les Juifs dans la catéchèse*, University of Louvain (1971–72). Gerald S. Strober, *Portrait of the Elder Brother* (New York: National Conference of Christians and Jews, 1972). Herbert Jochum, "Jesusgestalt und Judentum in Lehrplänen, Rahmenrichtlinien und Büchern für den Religionsunterricht," in the *Freiburger Rundbrief*, XXVI, nos. 97–100 (1974), 24–30.

cently issued a public warning in Jerusalem that the "heroic Jesus" presented in the schools today could pave the way for conversion efforts among the Jews by the ever-active missionary societies.

*　　*　　*

It is true that there has been considerable progress since 1945 in the Christian portrayal of both contemporary Jews and Judaism in the time of Jesus. But there is no denying that thirty years after Auschwitz much remains to be done. Herbert Jochum, professor and chairman of Catholic religion at the State Teachers Training Institute at Neunkirchen in the Saar, in his collection of studies, "Jesus' Relation to Judaism: The Image of Judaism in Christian Religious Education," points to specific dangers which the Catholic religion teacher should guard against: "In the opinion of the authors, at least, if one removes his Jewish background, then Jesus evidently undergoes a violent identity crisis. Under pressure to articulate the newness of the gospel and the special features of Jesus' message, and under the pedagogical necessity to do so clearly and convincingly, teachers unconsciously contrast Judaism with Christianity in a way that makes Jews the enemies of mankind. . . ." "The image of Jews, even of present-day Jews, which emerges in the minds of elementary school children, justifies the worst apprehensions. And thus in the end Jesus has to die not 'although he was a good man' but 'because he was a good man.' . . ."

"The Jews as legalists, as establishment types, contemptuous of human beings, are the Jews one needs if Jesus is to stand out as an iconoclast, an outsider, a humanitarian. Furthermore, there is danger that stressing the shocking and provocative elements of Jesus' activity will have no practical value for the outsiders of our society, but will only stir up feelings against members of the establishment and, once more, against the

Jews, encouraging renewed attacks on them as scapegoats."[11]
Might not the image of Jesus in the classrooms of Israel today
serve as a model of tolerance, to shape the image of Judaism in
Christian classrooms in a more truly Christian fashion?

11. *Freiburger Rundbrief*, XXVI, 1974, 29 ff.

III

Rabbis Speak of Jesus

Among the eighteen main names and titles which the authors of the New Testament give their Savior, "rabbi" occurs with special frequency—no fewer than thirteen times. Although in Jesus' day this term had not yet acquired the formal meaning of an ordained official, it was nevertheless already in common use as a title of honor for well-known Bible teachers and scribes. Not only his disciples (Mk 9:5; 11:21; 14:45) but others as well, Pharisees (Mk 12:14; Jn 3:2), Sadducees (Mk 12:18), and scribes (Mk 12:32), address him as "rabbi"—the Hebrew-Aramaic title is translated into Greek as "master" or "teacher."

The relations between the rabbi of Nazareth and his Pharisaic colleagues find their most authentic expression—before the editorial interference of Gentile Christian polemics, such as we see in the later Gospels—in the question of the greatest commandment: "And one of the scribes came up and heard them disputing with one another, and seeing that he answered them well, asked him, 'Which commandment is the first of all?' Jesus answered, 'The first is, "Hear, O Israel: The Lord our God, the Lord is one; and you shall love the Lord your God with all your heart, and with all your soul, and with all your mind, and with

all your strength." The second is this, "You shall love your
neighbor as yourself." There is no other commandment greater
than these.' And the scribe said to him, 'You are right, rabbi;
you have truly said that he is one, and there is no other but
he. . . .' And when Jesus saw that he answered wisely, he said
to him, 'You are not far from the kingdom of God' " (Mk
12:28–34). What comes out in this dialogue, which sounds
quite plausible historically, is above all the shared love for the
fundamental values of the Hebrew Bible and the mutual recognition of two rabbinical teachers.

*   *   *

Jesus taught many of the Pharisees of his day both in the Temple (Mk 12:35) and the synagogues (Mk 1:21 ff.; 6:2) of his
homeland. And despite profound differences of opinion, he
never denied their teaching authority but insisted, "Practice
and observe whatever they [the Pharisees] tell you" (Mt 23:3).
The general rabbinical attitude toward Jesus can be measured
by the fact that he was frequently a guest in the houses of
Pharisees (Lk 11:37; 14:1), that "some Pharisees" warned him
of Herod's plan to kill him (Lk 13:31), and that the "respected
member of the council" (Mk 15:43), the Pharisee Joseph of
Arimathea asked Pilate for the body of Jesus to give it honora-
ble burial according to the Jewish rite. It is also fair to assume
that a number of "rabbinical colleagues" joined Jesus' circle of
disciples, as Nicodemus the Pharisee did when he came to Jesus
by night and confessed, "Rabbi, we know that you are a
teacher come from God" (Jn 3:1–2).

The first Church, we know, was made up exclusively of faithful Jews, among whom were "a great many of the priests"
(Acts 6:7), a number of Pharisees (Acts 15:5)—i.e., rabbis—as
well as at least four ultraorthodox Israelites, who like Jesus himself (Mt 2:23) had taken vows as Nazirites (Acts 21:23; cf.
Num 6:1–21). Not only was Christianity founded by the first

community of Jewish believers in Jerusalem, which became the
mother Church of all Christians, but the gospel itself began
with the literary gifts of at least one rabbi—the author of the
so-called "proto-Mark"—who wrought Aramaic, Hebrew, and
perhaps even Greek materials into a rabbinical announcement
of glad tidings.[1]

But Matthew and Luke also show clear traces of tannaitic
ways of thinking, midrashlike biblical exegesis, and Pharisaic
methods of argument. These point unambiguously to rab-
binial sources of the text(s) on which they based their Gospels. As the surviving fragments of the Jewish Christian Gospels prove, Jesus was not viewed uniformly as a Great Man but
rather was interpreted charismatically in many different ways
by his followers (we cannot speak of Christianity in the modern sense within the various original communities). While one
group saw in him the prophet heralded by Moses (Deut
18:15), for others he was a perfect "just man," who alone could
keep the entire Torah. Still others understood him as a theological reformer, who had come to do away with the sacrificial cult
of the temple. At least two groups believed in him as the Messiah, for the present or the future. All these visions of Jesus
agree on his strong Torah piety, his religious mission to Israel,
his resistance to a mission among the Gentiles, and finally his
unequivocal humanness. The controversial title "Son of Man"
actually stresses this point, and it should have preserved him
from any posthumous deification.

"Hear, O Israel: The LORD our God is one LORD!" (Deut
6:4). This fundamental tenet of Israel's faith irrevocably links
both the Christ of Clement's letter (Hom. 3, 57) and the Jesus
of Mark's Gospel (Mk 12:29) to the traditional doctrines of his
people. This makes the fact all the more astonishing that Is-

1. For proofs of the rabbinical training of the author of "proto-Mark"
see Robert L. Lindsey, A Hebrew Translation of the Gospel of Mark (Jerusalem, 1969), pp. 9–65.

rael's most famous son, who led the West to God, has left behind in the annals of Judaism only isolated, obscure, and often negative traces. In talmudic literature, which stretches over roughly fifteen thousand pages, Jesus and his followers are the subject of barely fifteen pages. The blame for this anomaly must be placed mainly on a church which endowed Jesus with non-Jewish traits and made his name a weapon against Judaism. It victimized countless scapegoats from his people, fitting company for the "lamb of God." It laid the cross it was unwilling to bear on the shoulders of Jesus' brothers. It bound together its welfare with the misery of his people.

No wonder that harassed and persecuted rabbis could only respond to this Church, now the state religion of the Roman Empire and becoming continually more aggressive, with dignified silence. This discretion ought to have refuted the frequent charges by the bishops that Jesus was derided in the Talmud—charges that were often used as a pretext for bloody pogroms. Talmudic passages about Jesus, many of them deriving from his immediate environment, were mutilated, distorted, or obliterated by church censors, whose ignorance of Hebrew and Aramaic equaled their zeal for discovering "rabbinical blasphemies" against Jesus. Thus the so-called Ben Strada texts and other talmudic attacks on groups of Gnostic heretics who led a theologically hermaphroditic existence on the periphery of Judaism were interpreted by the medieval Church as slurs on Jesus, although there was no compelling reason to connect them with him.

This same medieval mentality was revealed by the monks who took part in a public disputation before the queen of France, Margaret of Provence, at Paris in the year 1240. The queen reprimanded them for "dishonoring their own faith, by claiming that such filthy things were written about Jesus in the Talmud."[2]

2. A. Lukyn Williams, *Adversus Judaeos* (Cambridge, 1935), p. 339.

What escaped the censor's scissors and the bonfires of Talmud burnings soon fell victim to rabbinical self-censorship. The rabbis prudently decided to nip in the bud any suspicion of "Jewish hatred of Jesus": "We forbid under penalty of the great anathema the publishing of anything in new editions of the Mishnah or the Gemara which refers to Jesus of Nazareth. Should this order not be scrupulously obeyed . . . that will bring still greater suffering upon us than in the past." So reads the declaration of the Jewish assembly of elders in Poland in 1631. Various rabbinical bodies immediately followed suit.

Nevertheless, scientific studies of Judaism have managed to restore a half-dozen credible passages about Jesus from Mishnah times. This pitiful gleaning makes it more than likely that Jesus originally had a much greater impact on rabbinical literature than the fragments we have today bear witness to. This becomes all the more evident when we consider the historical fact that during almost half a century, for as long as Jewish Christianity venerated Jesus in a way that was compatible with Jewish belief, the communities of his followers "throughout all Judea and Galilee and Samaria had peace and [were] built up; and walking in the fear of the Lord and in the comfort of the Holy Spirit [they were] multiplied" (Acts 9:31).

Only a faith in Jesus which observers within Judaism considered faithful to the Law—a sort of apocalyptic forerunner of Hasidism—could have gotten the defense which Gamaliel, the great rabbinical master of the Pharisees, made on behalf of the apostles of the new Church before the Sanhedrin: "Keep away from these men and let them alone; for if this plan or this undertaking is of men, it will fail; but if it is of God, you will not be able to overthrow them. You might even be found opposing God!" (Acts 5:38–39). So we read in the Acts of the Apostles, which also informs us of the success of this theological pleading: "So they took his advice . . . and let [the apostles] go" (Acts 5:39–40).

Today neither the Church nor the Synagogue can avoid the conclusion that whatever has withstood two or three thousand years of persecutions, aberrations, and allurements cannot simply "come from man." Since Judaism lives on in spite of Christianity, and Christianity goes on flourishing alongside Judaism, this coexistence must be God's unfathomable will. The first conflict arose when the rapturous vision of the divine Christ, deriving from Paul or Stephen and his associates, got the upper hand and in its Hellenized version shook the foundations of Jewish monotheism. For a Savior-God, who had to die amidst inhuman torments to atone on the cross for the sins of mankind, was in fact, as even Paul had to admit, "to the Jews a stumbling block" (1 Cor 1:23)—although for a rapidly growing multitude of Gentiles by no means "foolishness."

The divinization of a man, as far as the rabbis were concerned, was the essential scandal of all idolatrous cults. The revelation on Mount Sinai was meant to confute precisely this sort of thing. Even before the dispute over the divinity of Christ put rabbis on the defensive, it tore Jewish Christianity apart. For after the failure of his mission to the Jews (Acts 13:44-46) Paul renounced the "Jesus according to the flesh" whom he had never known (2 Cor 5:16), in order to make "another Jesus" (2 Cor 11:4) the core of his "gospel to the uncircumcised" (Gal 2:7). This differed as much from the "gospel to the circumcised" (Gal 2:8) of Peter (Cephas) and the other "pillars" of the first community (Gal 2:9) as the earthly Jesus who preached to the Jews differed from the supernatural Jesus whom the steadily growing Gentile Church now preached to the world.

The deification of Jesus by Paul and his followers inevitably had to lead to the demonization of Jesus in the legends of Jewish folk literature, which sought to caricature the evangelists' eulogy in a nasty lampoon entitled *Toledot Yeshu* (*The Gener-*

ations of Jesus).[3] Neither the Jewish gospel nor the no-less Jewish antigospel had the least intention of delivering an historically accurate report. What animated both of them was the power of faith. The first wished to spread the good news of Jesus, to lead Jews and Gentiles to salvation. The second wished to travesty the un-Jewish adoration of a murdered Jew so as to repel potential converts. Between these two antithetical Jewish images of Jesus stands the true, historic rabbi from Nazareth, who belongs neither in heaven nor in hell but on this earth—the goal of every effort of his all too brief existence.

However that may be, not even the crassest caricatures of Jesus in the *Toledot Yeshu* attempt what was achieved many centuries later by a number of Protestant theologians.[4] The *Toledot* neither denies the historicity of Jesus, nor conceals his miracles and cures, nor questions his Jewishness—for rabbinical law states that every son of a Jewish mother is a Jew.

In the face of this polarization in regard to the rabbi from Galilee, which soon recognized no middle ground between the "only begotten Son of God" and the "bastard in league with the devil," the picture of Jesus (as much as we have of it) presented in early rabbinical literature is surprisingly mild and benevolent. What has survived all the expunging and blotting out in those passages of the Talmud which almost certainly refer to Jesus is the memory of his ability to heal in the name of God, his manner of expounding the Scriptures, the fact that he left behind disciples, and an unhistorical, legend-encrusted tradition of his trial and execution.

For the Tannaites and later generations of rabbinical scribes Jesus is never the Son of God of Christian theology—a blasphemy against the Jewish understanding of God—nor the mes-

3. There is an extensive literature on the *Toledot Yeshu*. The best treatment is still S. Krauss's *Das Leben Jesu aus jüdischen Quellen* (Berlin, 1892).
4. For example, David F. Strauss, Bruno Bauer, John M. Robertson, Arthur Drews, Paul-Louis Couchoud.

sianic redeemer in an only too unredeemed world, nor again
the saving mediator between God and man, since this concept
contradicts both the power of repentance as described in the
Bible and the universal fatherhood of God. The incarnation,
original sin, Jesus' sacrifice of himself, and the Trinity—all
these concepts borrowed from Oriental cults and cultures remained alien to normative Judaism and taboo to the rabbis.
This rabbinical anathema found its polemical expression in
later levels of the Talmud, but it has nothing to do with the
historical Jesus of Nazareth. Only when the rabbis felt challenged to refute Pauline Christology can we detect an under-
tone of anger in their writings, but even then it is his worshipers, not Jesus himself, who are the target of their attacks.
Thus, as we have seen, Rabbi Abbahu writes about 270, "If
anybody says to you, I am God, he is lying; [if he says,] I am
the Son of Man, he will regret it in the end; [if he says,] I will
ascend into heaven, he will not do it."[5] Such attacks do not
refer to the pre-evangelical Jesus but to the Christ of the
Church Fathers, with whom some of the Talmud Fathers had
amicable theological debates. Only in the heyday of the gemara, when Jews and Jewish Christians fought each other all
out, as only those with the most intimate ties can fight over the
holy truths of faith, was Jesus accused of adulterating the Law
and leading the people astray. But he was never completely
rejected. In one rabbinical legend Jesus answers a certain Onkelos, who wishes to convert to Judaism, with a song of praise to
the Jewish people: "Now Onkelos conjured up Jesus from the
dead and asked him who was the most esteemed in the other
world. 'Israel,' answered Jesus. 'Should one join them?' he
asked. 'Seek out their best and not their worst. Whoever
touches them, touches the apple of God's eye.' "[6] These are
words of love, which might very well be an authentic logion of

5. P. Taanith 65b.
6. bGittin 57a.

Jesus. The rabbinical conclusion at the end of this didactic passage alludes to that feeling of love: "Now we can see how great the difference is between an apostate Jew and a Gentile prophet." Both sides considered each other apostates. Both were unshakably convinced that they were the true Jews, better than the others. But even in the most heated theological combat the other, the apostate, always remained a fellow Jew, undoubtedly mistaken but inalienably a son of David.

"Though he has sinned, he still remains a Jew!"[7] The majority of rabbis applied this guiding principle both to Jesus—that is, to the distorted Jewish and Gentile conceptions of him—and to Jewish Christians. The Gentile Christians were no theological problem for rabbinical Judaism. The basic formula was coined in the fourth century: "Among the Gentiles there are no heretics."[8] Up till modern times the Jews were a theological but never a political problem for the Church. Until well into the twentieth century exactly the opposite was true for Jews.

What emerges from the rabbinical polemic is the profile of a man—just as all the heroes and villains, all the saints and sinners of the Hebrew Bible are men. Now seen as a Pharisee, now an Essene, a reformer or a heretic, rebel, patriot, prophet, or impatient herald of the end of time, to mention only the most salient interpretations of Jesus, he appears as above all else a passionate Jew, often sounding like a Hasidic rabbi from Russia, whose love for God bursts through all the limits of human convention.

The oldest rabbinical passage which speaks of Jesus deals with one of the bright lights of the early tannaitic period, Rabbi Eliezer ben Hyrcanus, also named Eliezer the Great, whose magisterial opinions are quoted more than 320 times in the Mishnah. In two tannaitic texts,[9] which are thrice repeated

7. Sanhedrin 44b.
8. bChullin 13b.
9. Tos. Hullin II, 24, and bAboda Sara 16b.

with insignificant variations in later sources,[10] Rabbi Eliezer
praises a decision on religious law which was passed on to him
in the name of Jesus.

"When Rabbi Eliezer was arrested for heresy, they led him
to the place of judgment to pass sentence on him. The Roman
judge said to him, 'How can an old man like you bother with
such trifling things?' Eliezer answered, 'The judge is right.' The
Roman judge thought that Eliezer was talking about him,
whereas Eliezer was actually speaking of his Father in heaven.
Then the Roman judge said, 'Since you agree with me, you
shall be set free.' When Eliezer got back home, his disciples
came to him, to console him. But he refused all consolation.
Then Rabbi Akiba said to him, 'Rabbi, . . . perhaps you once
heard something heretical, and it pleased you. Perhaps you
were arrested on account of that.' Eliezer answered, 'Akiba, you
have just reminded me! Once I was going about the upper mar-
ketplace of Sepphoris, and there I met a disciple of Jesus the
Nazarene named Jacob, from the village of Shechania. He said
to me, "It is written in your Torah, 'You shall not bring the
hire of a harlot into the house of the LORD' [Deut 23:18]. But
may one use the harlot's wages to build a toilet for the high
priest?" "You have spoken well," I said, since at the time I could
not remember the Halakah. As soon as he saw that I agreed, he
added, "Jesus of Nazareth taught me that. Jesus was speaking
in reference to the prophet Micah, where it says, 'For from the
hire of a harlot she gathered them, and to the hire of a harlot
they shall return' [Mic 1:7]. Jesus added, 'It came from filth,
and it shall once again become filth.'" This pleased me, and
that is why I was arrested for heresy [or, Christian sympa-
thies]. . . .'"

In *Jesus of Nazareth* Joseph Klausner dates this incident
around 60 A.D. and identifies Jacob the disciple of Jesus with

10. Midrash Kohelet Raba to Eccles 1:8; Yalkut Shimoni to Mic 1, and
to Prov 5:6.

Jacob (James) the brother of Jesus (Gal 1:19). If so, this agraphon of Jesus would be older than the earliest Gospel, and it would be an instance of the popularity of Jesus' sayings, which are by no means recorded in their entirety in the New Testament, as Luke 1:1–4 and John 21:15 attest. But even in the case of a later date, say 80 or 90 A.D., which other scholars prefer, this saying would be at least as authentic as those in the Synoptic Gospels.

This remark of Jesus' about the harlot's hire, attested to by five rabbinical sources, permits us to reach some further conclusions:

1. It shows Jesus' typically Pharisaic method of exegesis, which, after the manner of his time, does not hesitate to reinterpret a line from the Torah in the light of a verse from the Prophets.

2. It shows Jesus' association with "tax collectors and harlots" (Mt 21:31; Lk 7:37–50), whom he looks after, trying to get them to return to the Torah. This is the ultimate reason for his pronouncing the harlot's hire relatively "clean."

3. It shows his earthy, often drastic language, likewise seen in strong expressions such as "whoring" (Mt 5:32; 15:19; Mk 7:21) and "belly" and "latrine" (Mk 7:19). He had to speak this way to farmers, fishermen, and "sinners," to illustrate the point of his ethical teaching.

4. It shows, as do so many canonical passages of the New Testament,[11] the veneration which Jesus felt for the central Jewish sanctuary, the Temple in Jerusalem. We know that, in keeping with the Bible, this respect included the priesthood, from the account of the cleansing of the leper to whom he says: "Go, show yourself to the priest, and offer the gift that Moses commanded,[12] for a proof to the people" (Mt 8:4).

11. E.g., Mt 8:4; 23:16–21; Jn 2:13–17; 10:22–23; Mk 11:11, 27; 12:41; 14:49.
12. Cf. Lev 14:1–32.

5. This halakic decision of Jesus' is a textbook example of the practical solution of a cultic problem hand in hand with the moral solution of an ethical problem. On the one hand, the question of where to relieve himself was an acute one for the high priest, since on Yom Kippur he had to remain in the Temple day and night or else incur ritual uncleanness. On the other hand, people in Israel did not share the Roman view that money had no moral color—they thought instead that sinful money could pollute even good things. Building a toilet for the high priest, not within the "house of the Lord" (Deut 23:19) but in one of the forecourts, was therefore a cultically useful answer to the question of how to spend the harlot's hire in a morally acceptable way.[13]

When Christianity became the state religion of the Roman Empire, there was no room in the Church for Jews. A dogmatism which would tolerate only one people of God, one kind of divine election, and a single way of salvation, condemned all Jews as murderers of Christ (Jn 19:5–18), who had "the devil for their father" (Jn 8:44). The rabbis were damned as well, lumped together as the "synagogue of Satan"(Rev 2:9; 3:9). In the period from the fourth to the sixteenth century no fewer than 106 popes and 92 Church councils issued anti-Jewish laws and regulations. Exile and mass murder, compulsory baptism and kidnapping of children, suffering and torture made Israel a martyr, a figure of affliction among the Gentiles, and its Diaspora a bloody, thousand-year-long Via Dolorosa.

So thorough was the extirpation of Jews that Duns Scotus, the *doctor subtilis* of the thirteenth century, seriously worried whether there might not be so few Jews left alive that "it would bring to naught their conversion at the coming of the Lord. . . ." There were times when the Church killed more

13. The so called "Temple roll" from Qumran, recently published by Professor Yigael Yadin, also gives precise details about the toilets which were to be built for priests and laymen in the vicinity of the Temple.

martyrs than it had produced—mostly among those whom Jesus had called "my brothers" (Mt 23:40). In the words of Karl Jaspers: "The only people who lived in the imitation of Christ all the way through the Middle Ages were the Jews." If not all Jews, certainly the rabbis.

Although Christianity had become a victorious, all-powerful state Church, it remained for the rabbis a marginal phenomenon, and they never actually developed an independent, reflective understanding of it. But for all that, one can hardly avoid the impression that the so-called Christian world of the Middle Ages felt compelled to wage a desperate struggle against a helpless Judaism. How else explain the fanatical zeal to convert Jews, the need, which so often strikes one as pathological, to triumph over the humiliated Synagogue, the carefully staged disputations, put on again and again by the princes of the Church with all their powerful secular resources, to force rabbis to confess that Jesus was the Messiah? Or was all this unchristian misuse of power only a narcotic to silence inner doubts, to drown out the suspicion that these Jews, despite all the humiliation and degradation, were the incarnation of the original Christian message, which people had long since given up listening to?

In any event, the rabbis had to vindicate themselves in these compulsory dialogues as best they might under the circumstances. In the main they had three arguments at their disposal:

1. To the charge that the Talmud defamed Jesus as a falsifier of the Torah, Rabbi Yechiel in the notorious Paris disputation (1240) conceded that the Talmud polemics referred to Jesus, "but not to Rabbi Jesus of Nazareth, who never rejected the Torah." The fact that Jesus (Yeshua, Yehoshua, Yoshua) was such a common Jewish name largely confirms this hypothesis. Josephus alone mentions a round dozen men who bore this

name,[14] while in the Talmud no fewer than twenty-one name-sakes of Jesus appear among the rabbis.

2. With regard to the legendary passage in the Talmud which maintains that Jesus was "hanged on the eve of the Passover" because he "practiced magic, led Israel astray, and divided her,"[15] Rabbi Joseph Albo said in the disputation at Tortosa (1413–14) that there was no evidence for these incidents, which already "lie so far back in the past." And "why blame present-day Jews for something which their forebears may have done many centuries ago?"

3. When Rabbi Moses ben Nachman (famous in scholastic Europe as Nachmanides) was asked for the thousandth time the question about the Messiah, in the disputation at Barcelona in 1263, he countered, "If our forebears, who were eye-witnesses of Jesus and knew him and his works personally, were nevertheless unwilling to believe in him, how can we accept the word of our king [James I of Aragon], who has no immediate knowledge of Jesus and is not his compatriot and contemporary? Does not the prophet say of the Messiah that he 'will have dominion from sea to sea, and from the River to the ends of the earth'? But Jesus entered into no dominion. Instead he was persecuted in his lifetime by his enemies and hid himself from them, finally fell into their hands, and could not save himself. How then should he save all of Israel? Even after his death dominion was not his, for the dominion of Rome was not on his behalf. Yet before people believed in him, Rome

14. Jesus the son of Phabi (*Ant.* XV, 322), Jesus the son of See (*Ant.* XVII, 341), Jesus the son of Damnai (*Ant.* XX, 203, 213), Jesus the son of Gamaliel (*Ant.* XX, 213, 223); Jesus the son of Gamal (*Bell.* IV, 160, 238, 316, 322, 325), Jesus the son of Sapphias (*Bell.* II, 599; III, 450–52, 457, 467, 498, etc.), Jesus the son of Thebuti (*Bell.* VI, 387–89), Jesus the son of Ananias (*Bell.* VI, 300–9), Jesus the rival of Josephus (*Vita* 105–11), Jesus the Galilean (*Vita* 200), Jesus the brother-in-law of Justus of Tiberias (*Vita* 178, 186), an unspecified Jesus (*Vita* 246).

15. Sanhedrin 43a.

ruled the largest part of the world. After they had embraced the faith, many kingdoms perished, and now the worshipers of Mohammed possess a kingdom which is greater than the Roman Empire ever was. . . . And has not your kingdom diminished, since it embraced Christianity?"

The third reply of the Spanish rabbi sounds like a timeless accusation of all pseudo-Christians: "And does not the prophet announce that in the age of the Messiah no one will teach another the art of war [Is 2:4] and that the world will be full of the knowledge of the Lord, as the waters cover the sea [Is 11:9]. Yet from the days of Jesus till the present the entire world has been full of murder, robbery, and plunder—and the Christians have shed more blood than any other people. . . ."

In his novel *The Last of the Just* André Schwarz-Bart describes one of the disputations where Christians asked the questions and rabbis had to answer, and the answer often spelled the difference between life and death. "At a question of Bishop Grotius relative to the divinity of Jesus, there was a rather understandable hesitation. But suddenly they saw Rabbi Solomon Levy, who had until then effaced himself like an adolescent intimidated by a gathering of grownups. Slender and slight in his black gown, he steps irresolutely before the tribunal. 'If it is true,' he whispers in a forced tone, 'if it is true that the Messiah of which our ancient prophets spoke has already come, how then do you explain the present state of the world?' Then, hemming and hawing in anguish, his voice a thread, 'Noble lords, the prophets stated that when the Messiah came, sobs and groans would disappear from the world—ah—did they not? That the lion and the lamb would lie down together, that the blind would be healed and that the lame would leap like— stags! And also that all the peoples would break their swords, oh, yes, and beat them into plowshares—ah—would they not?' And finally, smiling sadly at King Louis, 'Ah, what would they say, sire, if you were to forget how to wage war?'" The rabbi was burned to death—in the name of Jesus Christ.

* * *

Rabbi Saadia (882–942), head of the famous Talmud Academy at Sura in Babylon, was the first Jewish thinker to do a systematic analysis of the Trinity, which his predecessors had till then considered a Gentile version of tritheism and had ruled out of court. Saadia himself, like the Islamic religious philosophers, repudiates the "crassly materialistic Trinity, as understood by the masses"[16] and is likewise repelled by Augustine's images of the Trinity drawn from ordinary life. He discusses the inadequacy of all human speech, "insofar as it seeks to capture the ineffable God in words," and stresses the unity and uniqueness of God. His refutation of all dualisms and "concrete" Trinitarian doctrines reaches its climax in the presentation of his own understanding of the Trinity: "One can speak analogously of a man who declares that he does not adore fire, but merely the thing which burns, emits light, and blazes upwards—which is nothing else but fire."[17]

Saadia goes on to discuss a matter of law, whether Christians are to be considered idolaters since they adorn their houses of prayer with images of the diety and believe in the Trinity. He comes to the conclusion that Christians are to be esteemed "true believers in God," because the Trinity "of their intellectual elite" is nothing more than a sort of personification of the divine attributes of life, power, and knowledge, attributes which do not impair the unity of God since they are not meant to describe the essence of the deity but simply God's activity as we experience it. This decision has been accepted as binding by

16. *Kitab al-amanat wa-l-itiqadat* [Book of Beliefs and Opinions], ed. S. Landauer, pp. 85 ff. Cf. Jakob Guttmann, *Die Religionsphilosophie des Saddja* (Göttingen, 1882), pp. 101–7.

17. Ibid., p. 104.

almost all rabbinical authorities since the tenth century. Saadia deals with Jesus in connection with these theological arguments. In contrasting the Christologies of four different churches with each other, he postulates the impossibility of arriving at a single, uniform Jesus. He also attempts to disprove the claim that Jesus is the Messiah (in the Jewish sense) through fifteen refutations—five taken from the Hebrew Bible, five from history, and five from rational observation.

Without mentioning Jesus by name, Saadia describes—he is the first writer to do so—the Jewish eschatological legend of the Messiah from the House of Joseph, and of Armilos, who has been called, not altogether inaccurately, "the Jewish antichrist." In the fourth chapter of his major work, *The Book of Beliefs and Opinions*, we read, "[Our fathers] have also handed down to us . . . that a man will appear in Galilee from among the sons of Joseph, and men of the Jewish nation will gather around him. . . . This man will go up to Jerusalem after the Romans have conquered the city to stay there awhile. There he will be surprised by a man named Armilos, who will wage war on him and take the city, whereafter he will murder its inhabitants, dishonor them, and take them prisoners. Among those who are killed will also be the man[18] from the sons of Joseph."[19]

This midrash, which can be traced back through fragments to the second century, speaks in all its variants of a warlike Messiah, the son of Joseph, who will appear in Galilee and lead his followers to Jerusalem, where he will fall victim to an anti-Jewish Gentile ruler. In his wake the messianic king will appear, the son of David, to conquer his enemies at last and complete the process of redemption.

Whether this warrior Messiah has been modeled on the figure of Jesus—out of para-Christian, crypto-Christian, or anti-

18. An early ms. reads the title "Messiah" instead of "man."
19. Saadia, pp. 301 ff.

Christian motives; whether we should think of him as a product of national disappointment over the failure and death of
Bar Kochba, whom Rabbi Akiva in the second century declared
to be the Messiah; or whether the sharply contrasting features
of the different messianic traditions[20] required a doctrine of
two Messiahs—scholars are still arguing over all these possi-
bilities. In any case, the similarities in the origin, career, and
tragic end of both Galileans remain an inexhaustible source of
speculation.

That Galilee was the traditional starting point for most of
the Jewish wars of liberation is proved by an impressive line of
rebels, agitators, and would-be Messiahs. In 47 B.C., for example, a "robber captain" named Ezechias was executed along
with his band in Galilee by Herod. Forty years later a great
many Galileans under the leadership of Ezechias' son Judas of
Galilee took to arms in order, as Josephus says, "to seduce the
inhabitants into seceding" from Rome.[21]

Judas' motives and tactics remind one vividly of the methods
of Jesus, his Galilean countryman: "He held that it was crime
to pay taxes to the Romans and to tolerate mortal lords alongside God," writes Josephus.[22] "We have found this man perverting our nation," said the high priests and scribes to Pilate,
according to Luke 23:2, "and forbidding us to give tribute to
Caesar. . . ." But the parallel goes beyond this. Both Judas
and Jesus were called "scribes," which is equivalent to "rab-
binically trained Pharisees." Rabban Gamaliel, head of the
Pharisaic school and Paul's teacher, closely connects the work
of both men in the context of an anti-Roman uprising: "Judas
the Galilean arose in the days of the census [that is, of the tax
collection, which always stirred up opposition] and drew away

20. E.g., the redeemer "coming with the clouds of heaven" (Dan 7:13)
and the Messiah "humble and riding on an ass" (Zech 9:9).
21. *Bell.* II, 8, 1.
22. Ibid.

some of the people after him; he also perished, and all who followed him were scattered" (Acts 5:37). Gamaliel's "also" becomes clear only when we recall that Judas the Galilean anticipated Jesus' tragic fate in the insurrection of 6 B.C., while his sons Jacobus and Simon, the third generation of Galilean patriots, were crucified as "robbers" by the governor Tiberias Alexander around 46 A.D.[23]

We might also mention the Galileans whose assassination—probably as rebels—was reported to Jesus: "There were some present at that very time who told him of the Galileans whose blood Pilate had mixed with the sacrifices" (Lk 13:1). Galilee and Pharisaism, rabbis and Caesar's taxes, rebellion and the cross—the affinities are striking and ought to be more closely scrutinized.

*   *   *

Rabbi Solomon ben Isaac, the world famous Rashi (1040–1105), studied at Worms, where to this day a synagogue bears his name. According to an old Jewish tradition he supported himself and his family by growing grapes, so as not to misuse the Torah by earning his bread from it. His commentary on the Bible, which even now has lost none of its profundity and relevance, mentions "Yeshu the Nazarene" four times —mostly as a "magician" and a "perverter of the people." Here he was following an extracanonical tradition,[24] which projected the teaching of the Gentile Church on Jesus' divine sonship and the dogma of the Trinity (which to the Tannaim was polytheism) back into the life of Jesus in order to declare him, retrospectively, a heretic and "perverter of the people,"

23. *Ant.* 20, 5, 2.
24. E.g., bSanhedrin 106a and Yalkut Shimoni 766 to Num 23:7, as well as bSanhedrin 43a. Not without interest in this respect is the fact that Professor Morton Smith of Columbia University in a recent book (*The Secret Gospel*, New York, 1973) revives the theory that Jesus was a "soothsayer and magician."

and indeed in the sense of Deuteronomy 13:7–12 as someone who leads Israel to the practice of a "strange religion." All cures of the sick performed by persons suspected of heresy were looked upon as "sorcery"—although the Talmud also states that "Rabbi Yochanan said, 'For the Sanhedrin they only choose such men who . . . are wise and . . . are well versed in magic.' "[25]

Since by Jewish law the Synoptic Jesus can be considered neither an idolater nor a perverter of the people, much less a blasphemer against God, Rashi is denouncing not Jesus but, as recent studies have shown, the Christology of the Church Fathers.

Rabbi Joseph Kimchi (1105–70) wrote in his *Book of the Covenant* a model disputation between a Christian ("heretic") and a Jew ("believer"), in which the Jew refutes the Trinity, the incarnation, and Jesus' claim to be the Messiah on biblical grounds. Although Kimchi is prepared to recognize the Jewishness of Jesus, his knowledge as a scribe, and some of his miraculous cures, he rejects the doctrine of the two natures as contrary to the Bible: "If now, as you say, God has become flesh, did Jesus then possess the soul of God? If this is the case, why then did he cry out that God had forsaken him?[26] But if he possessed a human soul, and you do claim that the deity dwelt in him after his death, then whatever goes for the children of men is true for Jesus too."[27]

Kimchi's son, Rabbi David Kimchi (1160–1235), better known by the acronym Redak, in his polemical work *Answer to the Christians* gives the Jewish reply to the Christological interpretation of the Hebrew Bible. In his commentary on the Psalms he determines and corroborates the literal sense of passages such as Psalm 2:7 and Psalms 72 and 110 with a combina-

25. bSanhedrin 17a; cf. also Menahot 65a.
26. Mt 27:46.
27. *Sefer Ha-Brith* (Constantinople, 1750), pp. 27 ff.

tion of philology, history, and simple logic in an effort to dismantle allegorized "foreshadowings of Christ." In his vade mecum for polemical speakers, *Disputation*, he elaborates a detailed list of all the messianic prophecies which Jesus has not fulfilled "up to the present."[28] Typical of his clear, unambiguous argumentation are these words on the Nazarene: "Jesus himself declared that he came not to destroy the Law but to uphold it.[29] . . . Would it be compatible with God's all-mercifulness to let 3,500 years [since the creation of the world] pass without atonement until finally redeeming men from original sin through Jesus?"[30]

Around the year 1130 the Spanish-Jewish philosopher and poet Judah Halevi (1085–1135) completed his *Book of the Kusari*, the classic apology for the "despised religion." The book is cast in the form of four-sided conversation between a philosopher, a Jew, a Christian, and a Muslim. They are defending their religions before Bulan II, king of the Khazars, who has asked their help in his search for "the true faith." Apart from its elegant style and its truly ecumenical tolerance for all participants in the dialogue, the book is also notable for two remarks concerning Jesus which the author puts in the mouth of his "rabbi." In the first, Jesus is introduced as a disciple of Rabbi Yehoshua ben Perachia[31]—in keeping with a baraita which would make him a contemporary of King Alexander Jannaeus, more than a century before the generally accepted period when he lived.[32] Although Epiphanius makes reference to such a "proto-Jesus"[33] and the Karaite scholar al-Qirqisani represents Rabbi Yehoshua ben Perachia as the "uncle of Jesus,"[34]

28. E.g., Is 2:4; 9:6; 11:12; Zech 8:9; Ps 72:2–17.
29. Mt 5:17.
30. J. D. Eisenstein, *Wikkuach* (New York, 1928), pp. 60 ff.
31. *Book of the Kusari*, III, 65.
32. Baraita to bSanhedrin 107b.
33. *Haereses* (Dindorf edition), I, 486, and II, 81 ff.
34. *Jewish Quarterly Review*, VII, p. 687.

today a number of Judaists feel that what we have here is simply an error in Talmudic chronology. The great majority of the experts, however, consider the baraita legendary.

The second reference to Jesus has a Christological flavor. With profound grief Halevi describes the bloodshed and barbaric persecution of Jews by the Crusaders, as well as the mass murders triggered by them all over central Europe. In so doing, he interprets Israel's tribulations in the words of the suffering servant of God,[35] who brings the divine plan of salvation to fulfillment by humble self-denial. Looking for analogies to fit his case, he alludes to the first Christians, who bore "scorn and dishonor" with happy hearts, since after all "Humility and meekness are nearer to the divine presence than glory and sovereignty."[36] At the end Halevi's rabbi explains that "these communities of faith [Christians and Moslems] are making the way ready for the awaited Messiah, whom they will share along with the Jews. Then all three will become a single tree, as Ezekiel [37:17] once foretold their reunion in his ecumenical vision."

A worthy disciple of Halevi and one of the first Jewish ecumenists was the physician and philosopher Sa'd ibn-Mansur ibn-Kammuna (1215–85). His work on the philosophy of religion *Examination of the Three Faiths*[37] accepts divine revelation a priori as the basis of all three forms of monotheism. This rabbinical scholar was ahead of his time in his sober rationality, objectivity, and fairness no less than in his emphasis on the God-given humanity which inseparably unites Judaism and the Church. His paragraph on Jesus' miraculous cures reveals a characteristic respect for the "heterodox": "No doubt was entertained about the death and disease of those whom Jesus re-

35. Is 52:13; 53:12.
36. *Kusari*, IV, 22.
37. Moshe Perlmann, ed., *Ibn Kammuna's "Examination of the Three Faiths"* (Los Angeles: University of California Press, 1971).

vived and cured: it may be argued for the veracity thereof that
if anyone had had doubts it would have become known among
his enemies, Jews and others, in his time, and if it had become
known at that time it would have been reported. Doubts have
not been reported and, although some ascribed the miracles to
magic, or the devil's aid, or to Jesus having learned God's
highest name, it is clear that his contemporaries were certain of
the absence of illusion or collusion."[38]

After pointing out that not only Jesus but also the majority
of the early Christians remained devout Jews to the end of
their lives, he continues, "Jesus rose and washed the feet of the
apostles in water and said: 'The son of man has not come to be
served but has come to serve.' He never called himself a true
deity." On the other hand ibn-Kammuna takes contemporary
Christians to task in plain language. "In the Gospel it says: 'If
ye have faith as a grain of mustard seed, ye shall say unto this
mountain—Remove hence to yonder place—and it shall remove.' But we find none of the believers in Jesus able to move a
light stone or anything else."[39]

Moses Maimonides (1135–1205), the universal genius of the
Jewish Middle Ages, is "Rabbi Moyses" to Christian Scholastic
philosophers and the "Rambam" to Jews, to use the customary
acronym. His unique achievements in the fields of medicine,
philosophy, and grammar, but especially in biblical interpretation and codification of the law, have earned him the
accolade "From Moses [the lawgiver] to Moses [Maimonides]
there was no one like Moses." In his voluminous writings Maimonides comments repeatedly on Christianity and its founder,
frequently letting the polemical spirit triumph over objectivity.
The most important passage on Jesus occurs in his chief halakic
work, *Mishneh Torah*, in the eleventh chapter of the fifth part,

38. *Examination*, p. 99.
39. Ibid., p. 89.

on "Kings and Wars."[40] The text, however, has been so mutilated by Christian censorship that only a few editions of the
Hebrew text retain the author's authentic view of the role of
Christianity and Islam in the dissemination of monotheism
and the preparation of humanity for the messianic age. At bottom Maimonides agrees with Halevi's position on both religions derived from Judaism: "All these matters referring to
Jesus of Nazareth and the Ishmaelite [Mohammed] who came
after him only served to pave the way for the King Messiah,
and to prepare the entire world to worship God with one heart,
as it is written: [Zeph 3:9 follows]. In this way hope for the
Messiah, the Torah, and the commandments became a widespread common faith—among the inhabitants of the far islands
and among many nations, uncircumcised in heart and flesh."

Just as Pauline Christianity assigns a premessianic role to Judaism in God's plan of salvation (Rom 9–11), so both these
medieval Jewish luminaries saw Christianity—and Islam—as
part of salvation history, preliminary steps on the way to the
final redemption of mankind.

It is significant that Jews, who counted the authors of the
first Gospels among their ancestors, have read the New Testament with increasing frequency since the early Middle Ages.
Some may have done so out of curiosity, others for polemical
purposes, but at least one scribe—Don David Candia, in his six-
teenth-century manual, The Prosecutor's Evidence—used the
New Testament to turn the tables of controversy and rehabil-
itate Judaism with the words of Jesus and his apostles.

The first extant rabbinical tract containing extensive excerpts
from the New Testament in Hebrew—to carry the battle into
the enemy's camp—is Wars of the Lord by Rabbi Jacob ben
Reuben.[41] It contains the polemical counterpart to Justin Mar-

40. Mishneh Torah, Hilchoth Melachim, XI, 4.
41. Critical edition of Milchamot Hashem (Jerusalem: Judah Rosenthal,
1963).

tyr's *Dialogue with Trypho*, and is no less artificial in its
method and debating tactics. Its admitted goal is to disarm the
Christians and, wherever possible, persuade them of the truth
of the Jewish faith.

A typical example of the Jewish approach to religious controversy until late in the modern period is *The Shame of the Gentiles* by the philosopher and grammarian Profiat Duran, also
called Ephodi. It was written around 1397 to guide all Jewish
"disputants" in Spain. After documenting the internal contradictions and the deficient knowledge of the Old Testament
which he claims to find in the Evangelists, he makes a
thoroughgoing distinction between Jesus (a "foolish godly
man"), his disciples ("misguided"), and the Church Fathers
("misguided men who lead others astray").

Duran's attitude toward Jesus as a man and a scribe is quite
positive. Errors first began creeping into Christianity with the
apostles, who in their simplicity often misunderstood Jesus'
teaching, while the Church Fathers—especially Jerome—made
numerous mistakes in translation, mostly due to inadequate
knowledge of "Jesus' mother tongue." Among these errors, says
Rabbi Ephodi, belong Jesus' supposed claim to divinity, the
dogma of the Trinity, and Jesus' rejection of the Torah, "which
the Nazarene ardently wished to see upheld and perpetuated."

In this work as well as in his treatises on transubstantiation,
the sacraments, and the papacy, Rabbi Ephodi displays such a
comprehensive grasp of Christian dogma, from the New Testament to the decisions of the councils, that even today his critique of Christianity may be judged a useful contribution to
religious dialogue.

Unique in all the literature of medieval controversies is
Ephodi's open letter entitled "Be Not Like Your Fathers!"
which he wrote in 1396 to his friend David Bonet Bongiorno in
answer to his summons to convert to Christianity as he had.
This epistle is written with such subtle irony that for decades

the Church distributed it among Jews as Christian propaganda. When by chance someone saw through the piece and discovered the author's true intention—to glorify Judaism at the expense of Christian doctrine—all obtainable copies were hurriedly confiscated and burned. Brief excerpts from this circular letter will illustrate its stylistic agility: "Be not like your fathers, who believed in the one God. They spurned any notion of plurality in Him and misunderstood the sentence 'Hear, O Israel: The Lord our God is one Lord,' thinking that 'one' meant pure unity. . . . But do not do as they did. Believe rather that one is three, and three are one, innerly and essentially united. The mouth cannot express it, and the ear cannot comprehend. . . . Be not like your fathers, who busied themselves with speculation . . . and sought to establish the truth in this way. Do not do as they did! Far be it from you. . . . For you the truth must lie in this conclusion: The Father is God, God is the Son, consequently the Father is the Son. . . . Your fathers ate the bread of hardship, often went hungry and thirsty. But you have saved your soul, you eat and are filled with your Savior within you. . . . Be not like your fathers, who inherited Moses' teaching. . . . Do not do as they did; you would shame yourself if you did! Do not observe the commandments and prohibitions in the Bible! True, the apostles, as descendants of Abraham, observed its teaching exactly, even after the death of Jesus the Messiah and after they had been baptized in his name. But these and other contradictions you will surely untangle, for I know that the Holy Spirit speaks from within you, and nothing remains a mystery to you."

Another masterwork of this literary genre—the anti-Christian reaction to the flood of books by anti-Jewish theologians—is *The Book of Refutation*. It was written by Rabbi Shemtov Lippmann of Mühlhausen shortly after the Prague pogrom of 1399, after a disputation which he had been forced to take part in by a proselyte named Peter (alias Pessach) and the Church.

This Jewish *Summa contra gentiles* scrutinizes every controversial verse in the Bible, from Genesis on, to refute all the
Christological readings. The book is not without a biting
sarcasm—for example, in its comment on Genesis 1:26, "Let us
make man." Many theologians took the plural verb form as a
proof of the Trinity and of Jesus' divine sonship. After pointing
to the singular form of the following verse—"and God made
man"—Rabbi Lippmann scornfully concludes that "the Son
was obviously disobedient and made his Father do the work by
himself." That is why the Father "later abandoned the Son,
when he cried out for help on the cross."

In the Middle Ages practically all rabbis decisively rejected
any responsibility for the trial and execution of Jesus, not so
much for theological as for pastoral reasons, since the death of
Jesus all too often led to the murder of his brothers. The annual massacres of Jews on Good Friday proved this point with
lethal clarity. But for his part, Rabbi Lippmann not only ad-
mits the responsibility but declares—following Matthew 26:64
and Mark 14:62 ff.—that in keeping with Jewish law Jesus would
have been rightfully "stoned and hanged" for blasphemy.[42]
Since Rabbi Lippmann was well versed in the Gospels, as
shown by his penetrating critique of the New Testament, he
must have known that, according to all four Gospel accounts of
the Sanhedrin hearing, Jesus was in no way guilty of blasphemy. Hence his "confession" of the "murder of Christ" can
only be explained as all too human recalcitrance and as
defiance of church power and episcopal whim, which had
plagued him for years.

We can sense similar feelings in the words of another German Jew, who almost five hundred years later returned from
the brink of baptism to a more profound kind of Judaism than
he had left—Franz Rosenzweig. "We crucified Christ," he

42. In keeping with Sanhedrin IV, 4: "Only the Blasphemer of God and
the idolater are hanged [after being stoned]."

wrote, "and, believe me, we would do it again. We are the only ones in the whole world who would . . . should we ever again have to face the raging fury of idolatry, to stand before a multitude demanding the deification of a man."[43]

The first, and until very recently, the only Hebrew translation of one of the Gospels by a rabbi came from the pen of the Spanish Rabbi Shemtov ben Isaac ibn-Shaprut, who in 1375 had to defend his faith at a public disputation in Pamplona against Cardinal Pedro de Luna, who later became Pope Benedict XIII. At the request of many of his colleagues he put together notes on his theological strategy and polemical tactics in a detailed handbook called *The Touchstone* (after Is 28:16), since "it is meant to help distinguish truth from falsehood."

"I thought it good to round out this work with a translation of the Gospels, even though these books are strictly forbidden to Jews, for two reasons: first, to use them to answer the Christians with . . . and second, to prove to our brothers in the faith [here the church censor obliterated perhaps five words] . . . and so they will learn to their advantage [again, five or six words are missing] . . . how one can understand [three words erased] through the testimony of the other side. . . ."

Without "improving" the Vulgate text of Matthew, as did Jacob ben Reuben before him and others after him, ibn-Shaprut translates "simply and literally." He limits his personal viewpoint to the fifty-three "objections" which he interpolates between various episodes of the Gospel. "And I hereby implore all future copyists in the name of eternal life, not to transcribe this Gospel without writing in my objections as well, in their totality, word for word."

The task which Rabbi ibn-Shaprut set himself was not only linguistically difficult and without precedent on this scale but also essentially schizophrenic. As a believing Jew he could not

43. *Briefe* (Berlin, 1935), pp. 670 ff.

help sympathizing with Jesus' Sermon on the Mount, the "Our
Father," and the Jewish parables, such as those of the power of
prayer, the golden rule, and the evil of judging others. On the
other hand, the cries of woe upon the scribes and Pharisees, the
prophecy of the fall of Jerusalem, and the Christology of
Matthew arouse his anger. Jesus' refusal "to go to the Gentiles," his frequent stress on Jewish religious law, his profound
reinterpretation of the moral code, and the roughly seventy
quotations, references, and allusions to the Old Testament—all
these sound eloquent, natural, and fluent in ibn-Shaprut's Hebrew. Other passages, however—on the abolition of the cultic,
dietary, and ceremonial laws of Moses, the prophecies of doom
upon Israel, and the messianic claims of the Nazarene—sound
stiff and faltering.

This conflict between the Jesus of the logia source and the
Christ of Matthew is most clearly expressed in the notion of
the "Son of man." In Hebrew this is indistinguishable from the
simple "man," and so Matthew 17:22—"The Son of man is to
be delivered into the hands of men"—ends up sounding meaningless.

As an experienced Talmudist and controversialist, ibn-
Shaprut kept his feelings in check, but not always. His translation betrays contradictory biases, as when he re-Judaizes inexact
Old Testament quotations and distorted biblical references,
and again when he de-Judaizes Jewish formulas or turns of
phrase to which Matthew gives an antirabbinical or an-
tinomian slant. Despite all the Spanish rabbi's conscientious
striving for objectivity, both these tendencies are embodied in
the Touchstone in a manner which often reminds the modern
reader of Bultmann's school of exegesis.

There is a special interest in the one passage which ibn-
Shaprut completely misunderstood, Matthew 23:5—"They
make their phylacteries broad. . . ." At that time there was
hardly a scholar or a dictionary in the Christian world to trans-

late or explain for him the hapax legomenon *phylakteria*. So, groping in the dark, he inferred its meaning from context, combined it with the following verb, *magnificant* (approximately, "they adorn"), and the Hebrew result was "They wear expensive garments." This misunderstanding is not without a symbolic irony. The metamorphosis that the Jewish core of the "Good News" underwent in two successive translations—into Greek and then into Latin—had so wrenched it from its original setting that a pious rabbi could not even recognize his own tefillin, which he put on every day for morning prayers.

Despite these failings, ibn-Shaprut's Hebrew version of Matthew remained the best translation of the Gospel into the mother tongue of the Bible until well into the eighteenth century.

The image of Jesus in the Jewish Middle Ages is inevitably, given the spirit of the age, a dark one which, like a silhouette, displays its features in black. The rabbis were driven into a corner by a Church which forged the cross and the crucified into a lethal weapon, "to revenge the death of Jesus on the murderers of God," in the words of the Crusaders' battle cry in the Rhineland. In this situation the rabbis could only insist to the point of desperation on what Jesus was not and could not be for them. He was *not* the Messiah, since he had not even made this claim for himself. He was *not* the "only begotten Son of God," since all Israel had enjoyed this privilege since the exodus from Egypt (Ex 4:22 ff.). And he could *not* be the Savior of the world, since the inhuman acts of the Christians and the suffering they inflicted on the Jews were the most solid proof that the world had not been redeemed.

No wonder that faithful Jews tabooed the name of Jesus and spoke instead of "the nameless one" or "that man." When they had to use his name—as they were occasionally compelled to do by Church authorities—they transcribed it as the acronym of the biblical curse "Yimach shemo we-sichro"—

"May his name and his memory be blotted out!" (Ps 109:13 ff.; Deut 9:14). Thus a tormented minority found a way to vent its impotent rage. The Church's politics of hatred had gone so far that Jews learned to curse the Gentile caricature of another Jew.

In an attempt to remove the eternal apple of discord from Christian-Jewish disputations once and for all, Rabbi Joseph Albo (1360–1444) in his *Book of the Principles of Faith* struck belief in the Messiah from the list of the primary articles of faith. "The belief in the coming of the Savior," he maintains, agreeing with his teacher Rabbi Chasdai Crescas (1345?–1412), has been traditionally accepted by the Jewish people as part of their faith, "but it is not a fundamental principle."[44]

Speaking of the "Torah of Jesus," he writes that it is difficult to "establish the meaning of something expressed in the form of puzzles or parables"—unlike the Torah of Moses, "which speaks mouth to mouth, not through dark speech or parables" (Num 12:8). On the law of the Sabbath Rabbi Albo quotes Jesus in support of his charge that the pope has broken the ten commandments: "But even if we assume that the Apostles, as they claim, had the authority to alter certain regulations, who gave the pope the power to alter the Sabbath commandment, which does not belong to those statutes? . . . No one can do away with the Sabbath commandment, which is of divine origin, especially since it is one of the ten commandments. And it is a commandment which Jesus too, and all his disciples, observed for their entire lives."[45]

A good example of the way rabbinical apologists dealt with Christian "testimonia" (collections of Old Testament quotations which purported to predict the coming of Jesus), when intervals of tolerance on the part of their rulers made this possi-

44. *Sepher Haikkarim* [Book of Principles], text with English translation by I. Husik (Philadelphia, 1946), I, 186.
45. Ibid., 234 ff.

ble, are the counterarguments of Don Isaac Abravanel
(1437–1509), the last great Hispano-Jewish statesman and
thinker. Commenting on Psalm 72:8 and 11 ("He will have
dominion from sea to sea," and "All kings fall down before
him, and all nations serve him"), which the theologians wished
to refer to Jesus, he wrote, "Jesus did not rule over so much as
a village. On the contrary! He was persecuted by his enemies,
had to hide from them, and in the end fell into their hands,
without being able to free himself. After his death the sect of
those who believed in him had no power whatsoever. It was
Rome which had dominion over the world, both before and
after his baptism, although it lost considerable territory afterwards. Even in our days the Muslims, the sworn enemies of the
Church, exercise greater dominion than you Christians!"[46]

With the beginning of the humanistic movement and the
Reformation, a gradual liberalization of Christian-Jewish relations got under way, mainly because the center of gravity in
religious controversy had shifted to internal church matters.
Thus the Karaite Isaac ben Abraham Troki (1533–94) could
carry on a candid dialogue with members of various Christian
sects in Poland which is reflected in his work *Strengthening of
the Faith*. The peculiar feature of Troki consists in his systematic organization of objections to Christian theology and his
use of the New Testament as a source of arguments. Although
he was a Karaite—i.e., he rejected the oral tradition of the Talmud—his biblical exegesis bears a thoroughly rabbinical stamp.

In his critique of the theology of the cross, he states, "If
Jesus freely took the cross upon himself, and thereby the will of
God was done, then the Jews can only have been an obedient
instrument in the economy of salvation. Why therefore punish
the Jews for something which brought atonement and justification to all Christians? But if Jesus suffered death on the cross

46. *Die Quellen der Erlösung,* 41a.

against his will, then he can't be the God whom Christians worship and adore."

A *locus classicus* for ecumenically minded rabbis, since even before Christian times, is the obscure passage from the testament of Moses "The LORD came from Sinai and dawned from Seir upon them; he shone forth from Mount Paran, he came with tens of thousands of holy ones; in his right hand is a fiery law for them" (Deut 33:2). Rabbi Nathaniel ben Isaiah, a Yemenite scribe of the thirteenth century, in his Bible commentary *Light in the Darkness* proposed the following interpretation for these lines: "[The sense is] coming from Sinai, God sent prophets to Europe, both to the sons of Esau [Christianity] and to the sons of Ishmael [Islam], to offer them the teaching of his divine deeds. Some say also that Moses foretold the future to them, namely that Jesus would come to found Christianity, which would be incorporated into Roman Empire . . . and that faith in Christ would spread over almost the entire world, till the coming of the Fool [as Mohammed is often called in rabbinical writings, following Hosea 9:7] . . . and after him will come he of whom it is written: He comes with ten thousands of saints, that is the Messiah King."[47]

A similar interpretation of Deuteronomy 33:2 comes from Rabbi Abraham Farrisol (1451–1525), the author of the first account in Hebrew of the voyage of Columbus and the new world he discovered. Farrisol belonged to the group of luminaries at the Florentine court of the Medici. In his biblical commentary *The Shield of Abraham* he identifies Seir with Christian Rome and Mount Paran with the sanctuary of Islam, both of which became friction points for the kindling "of the flame of faith that has illumined the world."

Juda Leon de Modena (1571–1648) was a Venetian rabbi

47. Critical edition by Rabbi Kapach (Jerusalem, 1957), p. 29.

who apparently read the New Testament in Greek in order to compare it with the Vulgate. He wrote a manual for Jewish controversialists, whose Hebrew title, *Shield and Sword*, gives a clear indication of his strategy—a combination of self-defense and counterattack. In contrast to his fearless criticism of Christian doctrine, his approach to Jesus is marked by a sympathy which must have been looked upon by Jews of three hundred years ago as heretical. "At the end of the era of the second Temple, there were several trends in Judaism, which were all in accord with the Torah of Moses but disagreed in their interpretation of Scripture. . . . The Nazarene chose the best and most just among these trends, and followed the Pharisaic school. . . . Not only did he believe in the sacred Scriptures as the word of God but in the oral tradition as well. . . . He even said, 'Heaven and earth will sooner pass away than a single word of the holy Torah.' . . . I have not the slightest doubt that Jesus never under any circumstances claimed to be God or a part of the deity, as the Christians maintain, but as far as we can judge from his words and works such a thought never entered his mind."

In this passage and many others we may consider Rabbi Juda as the precursor of modern Jewish New Testament research, which has him to thank for a number of thought-provoking insights.

Rabbi Jacob Emden (1696–1776) is one of the most striking figures in eighteenth-century Judaism. He managed to combine an almost fantastic intolerance on purely Jewish religious issues with an open-minded rationalistic attitude toward his Christian environment. What can explain the respect—more, the frank sympathy—which he cherished for both Christianity and its founder? Certainly not the age he lived in, which still thought about Jews and their beliefs—and treated them—in a medieval fashion. Nor his German homeland, which penned him and his congregation in a dilapidated *Judengasse*, laid a head tax on

them like cattle, limited their livelihood to a few despised pro-
fessions, and even prescribed the number of children they were
allowed to bring into the world. Unlike his friend Moses Mendelssohn, he had no benefactors among the Christian elite, nor
did he seek influence with rulers as did the "court Jews" of his
time. His "Epistle on Tolerance," as Rabbi Oscar Z. Fasman
rightfully calls his collected writings on Christianity,[48] was written in Hebrew and aimed exclusively for Jewish readers. The
text speaks for itself and its author's sentiments: "The founder
of Christianity rendered a double benefit to the world. On the
one hand, he used all his power to reinforce the Torah of
Moses, for none of our wise men ever placed greater emphasis
on the eternal binding force of God's teaching. On the other
hand, he did the Gentiles a great service—if only they wouldn't
thwart his noble intention, as certain blockheads have done, by
not grasping the true sense of the Gospels—in that he did away
with idolatry, freed them from the service of idols, and obliged
them to observe the seven commandments of Noah . . . and in
fact he tried to make them perfect by means of a moral teaching which is still more demanding than the Torah of Moses."[49]

In his commentary on the *Sayings of the Fathers*, he makes
special reference to the guiding principle of Rabbi Yochanan
the shoemaker, "Every gathering in God's honor will endure.
The one which is not founded in God's honor will not endure."[50] It seems to be more than a coincidence that the Hebrew word for "gathering" used here, *knessia*, has acquired in
the colloquial language the meaning "church." In this sense
Rabbi Emden commented on it around 1757 in Hamburg:
"The gathering of the Gentiles in our days can likewise be

48. Oscar Z. Fasman, "An Epistle on Tolerance by a Rabbinic Zealot,"
in *The Jewish Library*, vol. IV: *Judaism in a Changing World* (London,
1971), pp. 93–105.
49. *Seder Olam Raba-we-Sutta* (Hamburg, 1757), pp. 35 ff.
50. *Abot* 4, 11.

characterized as a gathering in God's honor. It has the purpose
of announcing to the whole world that there is one God, who
is Lord of heaven and earth. . . . Therefore their church
[gathering] endures, because it honors the true God and His
Torah, and announces His Glory among the nations which do
not yet know Him. . . . Their merits will win a fitting reward
in heaven. . . . The house of Israel has received great consolation from them. . . . For if it had not been for the Christians,
our remnant would surely have been destroyed, and Israel's
hope would have been extinguished amidst the Gentiles, who
hate us because of our faith. . . . But God, our Lord, has
caused the Christian wise men to arise, who protect us in every
generation."[51]

Rabbi Emden's distinction between Judaism, the founders of
the Church, and Christianity, is theologically interesting: "The
founder of Christianity never had the idea of abolishing the
Torah, nor did his disciple Paul. . . . The disciples of the Nazarene chose baptism instead of circumcision for men who did
not wish to accept Judaism, and Sunday instead of the Sabbath
as the weekly day of rest, to testify that they were not fully Jewish. The Nazarene and his disciples, however, kept the Sabbath
most strictly and practiced circumcision, for they were after all
Jews by birth and descent, and observed all of the Torah. . . .
Christianity was only founded for the Gentiles."[52]

Rabbi Emden's remarks on Jew-baiters and anti-Jewish theologians have even today lost none of their relevance: "These
perverse scholars stir up great hatred against the children of Israel instead of inspiring the hearts of their people with love for
the Jews, who are truly devoted to their God. Since their
teacher [Jesus] bade them love their enemies, how much more

51. *Lechem Shamayim* (Hamburg, 1757), pp. 30 ff.
52. Ibid., pp. 35 ff.

should they not love us! O heaven, are we not your brothers?
Has not the same God created us?"[53]

Around the end of the Jewish Middle Ages, two voices made
themselves heard—not rabbis, but men who had gotten a rabbinical education in their youth: ". . . I do not believe that
any one save Christ alone ever attained to such superiority over
others as to have had the precepts of God which lead to ever-
lasting life revealed to him immediately and without the inter-
vention of words or a vision. . . . God manifested himself by
the mind of Jesus Christ immediately to the apostles, as he for-
merly revealed himself to Moses by the medium of the voice.
The voice of Christ, consequently, even as the voice which
Moses heard, may be called the voice of God. . . . But it is
necessary for me here to admonish my reader that I do not
speak either in affirmation or negation of those things which
some churches declare concerning Christ, for I freely confess
that I do not understand them."[54] Thus wrote Baruch Spinoza
(1632–77) in his famous *Tractatus Theologico-Politicus.*

A century later Moses Mendelssohn (1729–86) in his defense
of Judaism, which he viewed as "revealed legislation" and not,
like Christianity, as "revealed religion," cited Jesus of Nazareth
to bolster his thesis on the eternal validity of all the Sinai commandments. "Jesus of Nazareth not only observed the law of
Moses but also the statutes of the rabbis. If any of his recorded
words or deeds seem at first glance to run counter to this, that
impression quickly fades. If we carefully examine his life, we
find everything about it in complete agreement not only with
the Scriptures but also with tradition."[55]

If long afterwards the Gentile Church renounced its commitment to the Mosaic law, then in so doing it acted against the
will of its founder, as Mendelssohn gives us to understand: "In

53. Ibid., p. 37.
54. Unnamed translator (London: N. Trübner, 1868), p. 39.
55. *Jerusalem* (Leipzig, 1843), p. 357.

everything he [Jesus] did, just as in everything his disciples did
in the earliest days of the Church, we can clearly see . . . the
rabbinical principle: Whoever is not born in the Law may not
bind himself to the Law, but whoever is born in the Law must
live according to the Law and die according to the Law. If in
later times his followers thought otherwise and believed they
could dispense even the Jews who accepted their teaching, they
certainly acted without his authority."[56]

Both men were frequently urged to have themselves baptized, Spinoza by Pastor Heinrich Oldenburg and Mendelssohn
by the Zurich minister Johann Caspar Lavater. Both politely
but resolutely refused.

In nineteenth-century German Jewry there arose, hand in
hand with Jewish emancipation, a religious reform movement
which attempted to adjust theology to the new world where
Jews were citizens with civil rights. It aimed at reducing the
Jewish intellectual heritage to an indispensable minimum, so as
to assimilate Jews, internally and externally, as far as possible,
to their German fellow citizens. Thus the new Reform synagogues installed organs and introduced choirboys, dressed their
rabbis in robes, uncovered the heads of the congregation during
prayer, and permitted women and men to perform their devo-
tions side by side. They prayed in German, from an international prayerbook which no longer had either memories of the
Temple service or hopes for a messianic return to Zion. Liberal
Judaism, the fruit of the Enlightenment and its revolt against
Talmudic traditionalism, demythologized the faith of its fathers long before Bultmann, in order to crown "ethical monotheism" as a religion of reason. The key word of this new and
still uncertain theology was progressive revelation. Taking the
model of the continual flux of Darwinian evolution, divine revelation was reinterpreted as an unbroken process in which char-

56. Ibid., pp. 357 ff.

ismatic individuals could from time to time engineer a break-through to "the experience of God." Although such a theology of "open" revelation has the effect of relativizing most theoph-anies, it paved the way for the return of Jesus to the Judaism of his origins.

Abraham Geiger (1810–74), theosophist and reformer, defined the questions which the new Jewish theology had to deal with: "How did biblical Judaism reach the final stage where it is today? How did Pharisaic Judaism arise, and what basic motives co-operated in this process? Lastly, what was the makeup of the native soil from which Christianity emerged?"[57] Three years later Geiger, who was also a rabbinical scholar, went one step further: "It is obvious to the thinking Jew that early Christianity sprang up quite naturally out of Judaism, from the Jewish milieu of that time, the trumpet call of Jewish prophecy, and the Pharisaic struggles for liberation."[58]

This was a time when critical and historical studies of the Bible by Protestant scholars were casting doubt on a con-tinually growing number of church traditions in their still unfinished quest for the "historical Jesus." In their enthusiasm over this demythologization of Jesus, which had already begun with Reimarus (1694–1768), Jewish reformers saw in this new trend the confirmation of their own evolutionary historicism. For them not only was the Rabbi of Nazareth a legitimate sub-ject of Jewish research but he represented the promise of Chris-tian-Jewish collaboration. Out of this common effort Judaism, as the "origin and source" of Jesus, could only gain in social ac-ceptability. The negative Jesus of medieval Jewish polemics, created in self-defense, now became the positive Jesus of mod-ern apologetics, created in an act of Jewish self-assertion. In-deed one often has the impression that reformers who were try-

57. *Jüdische Zeitschrift für Wissenschaft und Leben*, 1867, p. 252.
58. Op. cit., 1870, p. 2.

ing with unseemly haste to strip their liberal faith of the accumulations of Jewish tradition were endeavoring with no less haste to re-Judaize Jesus—by means of the same Talmud and midrash which they largely repudiated in their own religious life.

And so, just when Ernest Renan (1823–92) and David Friedrich Strauss (1808–73) were depicting the antagonism between Jesus and Judaism, and Bruno Bauer (1809–92), a malicious enemy of Jews, was coming to the conclusion that the evangelists had simply invented Jesus, Jewish historians such as Isak Markus Jost (1793–1860), Heinrich Graetz (1818–91), and Abraham Geiger were turning to the Gospels to support their portrayal of Jesus as a Jew and to demonstrate that the source of his brilliance was the shining light of genuine Judaism.

It was as if nineteenth-century Jews were now eagerly striving to make up for the fifty generations of silence of their forebears. They released a veritable deluge of monographs, books, and dissertations on their long-neglected fellow believer. While this "Jesus wave" proved to be basically an effort to justify Judaism to outsiders, it showed nevertheless that Jesus could only be understood in his original Jewish context and that neither his sense of himself nor his message could be discussed in terms of the false dichotomy "Jesus or Judaism."

So it was that Samuel Hirsch (1808–89), a Reform rabbi and Hegelian philosopher, could move from the rabbinate in Dessau to the presidency of the Reform Rabbinical Assembly of America (1869) without anyone taking offense at his passionate interest in Jesus or finding it incompatible with his office. In his long-winded book *The System of the Religious Concepts of the Jews and its Relation to Christianity, Paganism, and Absolute Religion,*[59] he devotes an exhaustive analysis to the Naz-

59. Frankfurt-am-Main, 1842.

arene. Jesus was for him not merely a Jew but "the only Jew" in fact who had succeeded in realizing "the intense religiousness" of his faith. His greatness consisted in the fact that he "had grasped the idea of Judaism in all its profound truth, had been grasped by it, and began to live it in exemplary fashion."[60]

Jesus was interested only in his fellow Jews. He wanted to make them "the salt of the earth," for "what all Israel must do, every individual Jew must do as well," so that the promised kingdom of God might finally come. "The suffering servant of God," who in his total self-denial is to bring on the kingdom of heaven, is the expression of this radical Jewish demand, which will have nothing to do with half measures. Entirely geared to the Jewish people, he recognizes only those Jews who are his spiritual kin. They are to support him, the son of God (not the only begotten!), in the primary Hebrew sense of this biblical title of honor, in his work of redemption. His mistake in believing in the imminent dawning of the kingdom of God in no way separates him from Judaism. On the contrary, it proves his authentic Jewish drive to better the world and his impatient longing for the messianic consummation.

Lest the power of Jesus' hope and his spiritual greatness end with his death, God inspired the band of his disciples with the notion that he arose from the dead and was still alive. "In fact he really does live on in all those who wish to be authentic Jews." Rabbi Hirsch is so strongly convinced that Jesus and the teachings of Judaism are synonymous that he takes every departure from Jewish tradition in the Gospels for a later interpolation by the Gentile Church. He assigns sole responsibility for Christianity's permanent separation from Judaism to Paul, who transformed Jesus into a "metaphysical entity."[61] Nonetheless,

60. Ibid., ch. V, pp. 687 ff.
61. Ibid., pp. 767 ff.

Christianity's chief task of "spreading the idea of Judaism among pagan peoples" is still a binding divine mandate.

While scarcely a single Christian theologian was ready to concur with this rapturous "recovery of Jesus," no student of religion could disagree with the opinion of the Orthodox head rabbi of Vienna, H. P. Chajes: "It is very much to be regretted that Jews were unable to participate in research on Christian origins. Unfortunately, a wall of hostility always stood between the Jews and their offspring, the Christians. . . . Only in the last few decades do we observe some modest attempts by Jews to join in this scholarly task. . . . You have to be a rabbinical Jew, to know midrash, if you wish to fathom the spirit of Christianity in its earliest years. Above all, you must read the Gospels in the Hebrew translation. When you do, certain aspects of the text which non-Jewish scholarship is hardly aware of become immediately apparent. . . . Jews have the obligation of collaborating in New Testament research, if only because this will be of great service to their own scientific studies. One may safely predict that non-Jews will not be able to handle this momentous task, for you have to have Palestinian Judaism of the early Christian period in your head and in your blood if you want to measure up to this sort of research."[62]

In modern times many Jewish scholars have attempted to fill in the gaps in the Church's dogmatic presentation of Christ with their new image of Jesus the Jew. Often it was only a short step from the Viennese head rabbi's lofty call to scholarly co-operation (he himself made more than a dozen significant contributions to research on Jesus) to the war cry of someone like De Jonge: "Get out of the Gospels, you pastors! Hands off Yeshua! . . . Bring your booty here! . . . Yeshua the Jew!"[63]

62. "Jüdisches in den Evangelien," dated November 6, 1919, in *Reden und Vorträge*, ed. Moritz Rosenfeld (Vienna, 1933), pp. 271 ff.

63. M. De Jonge, *Jeschua, der klassische jüdische Mann: Zerstörung des kirchlichen, Enthüllung des jüdischen Jesusbildes* (Berlin, 1904), p. 100.

Elia Benamoseg (1822–1900), an Orthodox rabbi from Livorno and director of the best known rabbinical seminary in Italy, tried to find the golden mean in this question. In his comparative study *Jewish and Christian Morality*[64] he proves from rabbinical sources that Jesus' teaching was fundamentally Pharisaic—so much so that Jesus became "the Benjamin of the Pharisaic school." He then proceeds to the unequivocal conclusion: "It is therefore not surprising that Jesus and Christianity preach a just, liberal, and broad-minded morality."[65]

After illustrating most of the parables and ethical imperatives of the gospel with parallel passages from the Talmud, he goes on to say, "When Jesus spoke these words, he was in no way abandoning his Judaism. He preaches no strange or unfamiliar doctrine but aligns himself squarely with the two leading Pharisaic schools."[66]

In his late ecumenical work *Israel and Humanity*,[67] published posthumously, he stresses that "Jesus never wanted to found a new school or religion, nor did he have the slightest notion of the religious movement which came into being much later in his name."[68]

The first modern commentary on the Gospels in Hebrew was written by an Orthodox rabbi, Dr. Elie Soloweyczyk, and published in Paris in 1875.[69] The main concern of this work, which was translated by Rabbi L. Wogue into French, and later translated into German under the title *The Bible, the Talmud, and the Gospel*, is to establish the fundamental identity of Jewish and Christian ethics: "Jesus had no other end in view than to animate men with faith in the one God and to urge them on to

64. Paris, 1867.
65. Ibid., p. 159.
66. Ibid., p. 209.
67. Paris, 1914.
68. Ibid., p. 284.
69. *Kol Koré o Ha-Talmud Wehabrith Hachadashah.*

the practice of all the neighborly virtues and love for everyone, even enemies. May God grant us all, Jews and Christians, that we may follow the teaching of Jesus and his shining example, for our well-being in this world and our salvation in the next. Amen."[70]

In explicating Peter's confession "You are the Messiah!" (Mt 16:16), Rabbi Soloweyczyk suggests that "Peter was simply trying to express in strong language how magnificent Jesus was: Thanks to your extraordinary virtues you are indeed the anointed one, chosen by God; and you deserve to be called not only son of man but also son of God—a phrase which, as we have repeatedly shown, is used in both Testaments to designate the truly just man."[71]

German Jews were among the first victims of the reactionary oppression which followed the revolutionary wave of 1848, and were likewise in the vanguard of the emigration which brought German and Jewish ideas to North America. Encouraged by the generosity of their new environment—and its lack of history—the Jewish Reform movement took hold immediately. And thus began an unprecedented jettisoning of tradition to make room for new customs, concepts, and interpretations.

In the effort to catch up with, if not outstrip, the Protestant demythologizers, only one American Reform rabbi went as far as Bruno Bauer, Lessing, Renan, Voltaire, and other "Christian" representatives of a radical school of biblical criticism which called the authenticity of Jesus into question. In the person of Isaac Mayer Wise (1819–1900), who served as a Reform rabbi in Cincinnati from 1854 on, the "Progressives" found not just a powerful speaker but an organizational genius. As newly elected president of the Central Conference of American Reform Rabbis he managed to build this new school of Judaism into a full-fledged institution.

70. Ibid., III, 9.
71. Ibid., I, 294.

In his book *The Martyrdom of Jesus of Nazareth*[72] he devotes a passionate chapter to proving that "the Jews did not crucify Jesus,"[73] since the Romans clearly "have to bear the sole responsibility for this judicial murder." "The pack of howling fanatics," he continues, "who still cry at the heels of the Jew, 'Christ Killer,' have yet to learn to read and understand the gospels correctly."[74]

In the explosive finale of his book Wise gives vent to all the pent-up frustrations of the Middle Ages: "The Christian story, as the gospels narrate it, is a big bubble. You approach it critically and it bursts. Dogmatic Christology built upon it is a paper balloon kept afloat by gas. All the so-called lives of Christ, or biographies of Jesus, are works of fiction, erected by imagination on the shifting foundation of meager and unreliable records. . . . The trials of Jesus are positively not true: they are pure inventions. The crucifixion story as narrated is certainly not true, and it is extremely difficult to save the bare fact that Jesus was crucified. . . . We challenge all orthodoxy to produce from the gospels any sound, humane, and universal doctrine not contained in our 'Judaism.' . . . The universal, religious, and ethical element of Christianity has no connection whatever with Jesus or his apostles. . . . In the common acceptation of the terms, one can be a good Christian without the slightest belief in Jesus or the gospels. . . . In this third quarter of the nineteenth century the intelligence believes no longer in Jesus or the gospels. . . . The decline of the Church as a political power proves beyond a doubt the decline of Christian faith. . . ."

Next, the rabbi attacks the orthodoxy of both Church and Synagogue—in the same breath: "Like rabbinical Judaism, dogmatic Christianity was the product of ages without typography,

72. Cincinnati: Office of the American Israelite, 1874.
73. Ibid., p. 129.
74. Ibid., p. 131.

telescopes, microscopes, telegraphs, and the power of steam. These right arms of intelligence have fought the titanic battles, conquered and demolished the ancient castles, and remove now the debris, preparing the ground upon which there shall be reared the gorgeous temple of humanity, one universal republic, one universal religion of intelligence, and one great universal brotherhood. This is the new covenant, the gospel of humanity and reason."[75]

Nine years later Wise, who had meantime grown older and more cautious, published a revised interpretation of the Nazarene. In *Three Lectures on the Origins of Christianity*[76] the rabbinical fire-eater sounds somewhat mellower: "Jesus of Nazareth was not the founder of Christianity. He was a Pharisaic scribe and a Jewish patriot who was firmly resolved to free his homeland from the claws of a bloody tyranny. . . . For this reason he was hated by the Roman authorities and their Jewish sympathizers in Judea. When he was proclaimed Messiah, his death became inevitable. . . . He had not come to start a bloody revolution, for he knew that any attempt of this sort could only end in catastrophe. When the moment came, he sacrificed himself to protect his own. He said that he had only been sent to the lost sheep of Israel—and this mission cost him his life."[77]

If a Reform rabbi tried for a while to question the authenticity of Jesus' life, it was the head rabbi of Sweden, G. Klein, who "gave the decisive word in the debate on the historicity of Jesus, and disarmed all the sceptics."[78] In a thin little volume, provocatively entitled *Is Jesus a Historical Personality?*[79] he

75. Ibid., p. 134.
76. Cincinnati, 1883.
77. Ibid., pp. 7 ff.
78. Gösta Lindeskog, *Die Jesusfrage im neuzeitlichen Judentum* (Uppsala, 1938), p. 206.
79. Tübingen, 1910, 46 pp.

maintains that in the Gospels "a Jew is speaking, no cult hero but a Jew with a marked national consciousness."[80] After a rabbinical exegesis of the three Synoptic Gospels, Klein draws the following conclusion: "The background is definitely Jewish. The odor of the Palestinian earth which streams up from these pages is so strong that only unbridled fantasy could transform this historical Jesus into a myth."[81]

One of the reasons which brought Rabbi Klein to this conviction was the Sanhedrin trial, which "had to condemn Jesus to death" since he had in fact "committed blasphemy." Klein's argument contradicts almost all Jewish and many Christian interpretations, which see in the entire Sanhedrin section the tendentious interpolation of a later generation, but his reasoning is not without a certain originality: "In this context I also want to say a word about the reasons for the condemnation of Jesus. The sources state that this took place on account of blasphemy, but nowhere do they specify what this crime consisted in. For the answer which Jesus gives the high priest would never have been considered by a Jew of his time as a blasphemy against the divine name. . . . Nothing could offer more pointed proof of the historicity . . . of his condemnation than the conversation between Jesus and the high priest—provided that we understand it rightly. In Mishna Sukka IV, 5, there is an account of the procession around the altar at the feast of Tabernacles: Every day of the feast they walked in procession around the altar, reciting the prayer: Ah, God, help! [Ps 118:25] Rabbi Yehuda said: They prayed Ani-We-Hu, O help! In this Ani-We-Hu I find the 'secret name of God,' which Jewish tradition says God will reveal to all men in the time of the Messiah. One Mishna teacher explains the matter in this way: Ani-We-Hu = I and He = I want to be like Him. As He is merciful and loving, so I too want to be merciful and loving. That is the mean-

80. Ibid., p. 27.
81. Ibid., p. 28.

ing of the hidden name of God. It conceals within itself the deepest mystery of religion, the *unio mystica*, the demand that we become one with God. Jesus came to reveal this mystery to the world. When he utters those powerful, but usually misunderstood, words 'I and the Father are one' [Jn 10:30], he is thereby expressing the meaning of the secret name of God. This teaching pervades the entire fourth Gospel.[82] So I contend that Jesus' opponents had in their own eyes a solid reason for accusing him of the sin of blasphemy. For he was treated as a blasphemer on account of his uttering the 'secret name of God,' which in their opinion he had no right to do. And the statute on blasphemers in Mishna Sanhedrin VII, 5, reads: 'The blasphemer only incurs guilt if he utters the secret name of God. . . . When this sentence is pronounced . . . the judges arise and rend their garments and never again sew up the torn parts.'

"Concerning Jesus' conversation with the high priest, we read the following in Mark 14:61: 'Again the high priest asked him, "Are you the Christ, the Son of the Blessed?" and Jesus said, "I am. . . ."' In all probability, Jesus' answer in the Hebrew text was *Ani-We-Hu*. The evidence for this is the next line in the story, 'And the high priest tore his mantle, and said, "Why do we still need witnesses? You have heard his blasphemy."' The tearing of the garments only occurred upon hearing the name of God pronounced. Consequently Jesus uttered this name, and thus the high priest had an apparently sound legal argument for condemning him. He had attained his goal: he was justified before the people, and Pilate could take care of the rest."[83]

After further developing his rabbinical arguments, Klein comes to his final summary: "Let me summarize my conclusions, reached after more than three decades of studying the

82. Cf. Jn 9:15; 5:19 ff.; 41:10 ff.; 17:6 ff.
83. Ibid., pp. 41 ff.

history of New Testament times: No teaching has been handed
down to us from antiquity bearing a clearer and more incisive
personal stamp than the teaching of Jesus or, to use Harnack's
term, the 'first Gospel.' In it we see and hear a well-defined personality, with all the features appropriate to his time—and
Jesus can only be explained within the framework of his time
and environment. It is pointless to look anywhere else for the
kind of ethical monotheism which Jesus preached, in the Spirit
and in unison with the prophets of Israel. Pointless to look anywhere else than the world of Jewish thought in which Jesus
moved. Here is a fact which rests on so firm a foundation that
no philosophy can shake it: Jesus of Nazareth is a historical
personality."[84]

Most of the rabbinical treatments of Jesus in the last hundred years go further than this. They have a certain iconoclastic
intent—the de-Hellenizing and re-Hebraizing of the man who
is called "rabbi" no fewer than a dozen times in the New Testament. To this day the Grecisms in its approach to Jesus and
his message represent the basic evil of the Gospels to most
rabbis, just as in Jesus' day the same Hellenism represented to
their Tannaite predecessors the revolting antithesis of everything that Judaism stood for.

"Jesus was a Jew, Hebrew of Hebrews. Whatever I believe
with respect to the imputed miracle of his birth, his mother,
Mary, was a Jewish woman. He was reared and taught as a Jew.
He worshipped in the synagogue. He spoke no language save
Hebrew. . . . Jesus did not teach or wish to teach a new religion." This paragraph from the autobiography of one of the
most popular Jewish spokesmen in America, Rabbi Stephen
Wise,[85] is almost completely in accord with all modern rabbinical readings of Jesus—with one notable exception: Aron

84. Ibid., pp. 45 ff.
85. *Challenging Years: The Autobiography of Stephen Wise* (New York:
Putnam, 1949), p. 281.

(Armand) Kaminka (1866–1932), an Orthodox rabbi in Vienna, founder and head of the renowned Maimonides Institute in the Austrian capital, wrote a little book[86] about the pseudonymous Talmudic legend which denies Jesus' Jewish descent.[87]

Rabbi Kaminka refers to Isaiah's description of Galilee as "land of the Gentiles" (Is 9:1), to the derogatory allusion in the first book of Maccabees to "Galilee of the heathens" (1 Macc 5:15), to the "anathema of uncleanness" which Rabbi Yose ben Yoeser and Rabbi Yose ben Yochanan pronounced over "the land of the Gentiles,[88] and to various other rabbinical writings. His conclusion: "The entire country of Galilee . . . had as a matter of fact ceased to belong to Israel. . . . Galilee remained as pagan as ever, inhabited by a mixed population."[89] The book ends with some thoughts on the Messiah which strike one as almost racist: "Fanatical spirits of non-Jewish extraction, such as Paul of Tarsus and others, might well abandon their Gentile homeland. They might then go to Jerusalem and acquire certain ideas there, paying no attention to the qualified exponents of these ideas. And they could proclaim them to citizens of the Empire, preaching of justice and grace, guilt and reconciliation. But the Jewish race was awaiting a messianic upheaval, not just the appearance of a striking personality (and least of all of an alien personality). It was awaiting at the same time the glorification of its national identity, since its continued existence as the chosen people is its only dogma and the foundation of its belief in divine authority or revelation. If Israel could not think of rising up and conquering

86. *Studien zur Geschichte Galiläas* (Berlin, 1890).
87. In the so-called Ben-Stada allusions, as, for example, in bSabbath 104b and bSanhedrin 67a, which have been recognized since the twelfth century as having no connection with Jesus.
88. bSabbath 14–15.
89. *Studien zur Geschichte Galiläas*, p. 30.

its enemies because of its lack of military strength, there remained one all-important task: to maintain itself, to persevere in its eternal indissolubility, for its own sake, even if it could not yet take its place alongside or above the nations of the Gentiles, and to keep the expectation alive that the salvation of mankind must come forth from Zion and Jerusalem, and from Jewish blood."[90]

Nine years later the idea that Jesus was not truly Jewish was fastened on by a man who had chosen to become German, Houston Stewart Chamberlain. Chamberlain's goal was to make his "scientific" anti-Semitism generally acceptable, even to Christian circles in Germany. "Whoever maintains that Jesus was a Jew," he wrote emphatically, "is either ignorant or dishonorable."[91] The thesis which "proved" that more Aryan than Jewish blood flowed in Jesus' veins rapidly found adherents in Germany. "Jesus was not really a Jew; he was a Galilean, which is not the same," wrote Pastor H. Monnier,[92] who relies on Rabbi Kaminka's sources, though he does not quote Kaminka himself. Monnier claims that owing to the "predominantly Gentile population of Galilee," it seems plausible that Jesus was born a "half-breed." From here it was only a short step to make Jesus the son of a German soldier and a Persian mother, as Wilhelm Hauer proposed,[93] while Walter Grundmann taught (at Jena, in 1941) that Jesus' mother came "from the Gentiles," thus removing a "racial burden" from her son.

Just as the Jewishness of Jesus was used as a murder weapon against Jews in the Middle Ages, so the neopagans of our century had to make a public display of undoing that Jewishness before preparing the greatest mass Golgotha in world history for his brothers and sisters.

90. Ibid., p. 58.
91. *Die Grundlagen des 19. Jahrhunderts* (Berlin, 1899).
92. *Die historische Mission Jesu* (1906), p. 27.
93. *Ein arischer Christus* (Karlsruhe, 1939).

Rabbi H. G. Enelow (1877–1934), like his Orthodox colleague Kaminka, underscored the importance of Jesus' Galilean origins, but came to a completely different conclusion. Since Galilean Jews were exposed to much stronger Gentile influences than their fellow believers in Judea, they were less inclined to "rigid orthodoxy" and more "open-minded" in their attitudes towards religious law. Hence too they showed a greater readiness to welcome charismatic leaders and "prophetic personalities." For Enelow, an American Reform rabbi, Jesus is the prototype of "the supreme Jewish idealist," who recognizes no material difficulties when it comes to promoting his lofty goal: "The Kingdom of God, he decided, was not political, it was not of this world: it was spiritual. . . . As for himself, he decided, if to realize inwardly the kingdom of God meant to be the Messiah, the Anointed of God, God's Son, he was the Messiah. . . . The rulers, hearing that he had proclaimed himself Messiah, and having had experience with other self-styled messiahs, decided to hand him over to the Roman authorities, lest the whole people be charged with rebellion. They were not in a mood—perhaps they had no taste—for fine spiritual analysis. Thus, Jesus lost his life in the messianic maelstrom of his age."[94]

Rabbi Enelow, who later became president of the Central Conference of American Reform Rabbis, explains the Jewish silence on Christ in a pregnant sentence: "When we think of what doctrines were founded on the life and words of Jesus subsequently, and to what treatment of the Jews the religion named after him lent itself, we can understand why so little attention was paid to Jesus in the course of Jewish history."[95]

Now, however, the situation has improved. ". . . the modern Jew realizes the ethical power and spiritual beauty of Jesus. In

94. *A Jewish View of Jesus* (New York: Macmillan, 1920), pp. 130, 132.
95. Ibid., p. 166.

this regard Jesus takes his place among the noble teachers of
morality and heroes of faith Israel has produced."[96]

The book ends on a hopeful note: "Among the great and the
good that the human race has produced, none has even ap-
proached Jesus in universality of appeal and sway. He has become the most fascinating figure in history. In him is combined
what is best and most mysterious and most enchanting in Israel
—the eternal people whose child he was. The Jew cannot help
glorying in what Jesus thus has meant to the world; nor can he
help hoping that Jesus may yet serve as a bond of union between Jew and Christian, once his teaching is better known
and the bane of misunderstanding at last is removed from his
words and his ideal."[97]

The story of Joseph Krauskopf is a strange one. He was an
American Reform rabbi who, on the advice of his wife, at-
tended the Oberammergau Passion Play in the summer of
1901. During the three torturous, tedious acts of the amateur
drama, two contradictory feelings, he said, struggled in his
heart: revulsion at the malicious way the Bavarian villagers car-
icatured Jews and Judaism, and a growing sympathy for the
hero of the seemingly endless performance. "I know of nothing
that could have rooted deeper, among these people, the existing
prejudice against the Jew, and spread wider the world's hatred
of him, than this Passion Play of Oberammergau,"[98] he wrote
the next day. As soon as the curtain fell after the crucifixion, he
sketched out the first draft of a book which was to nourish
Rabbi Enelow's utopian hopes: "It is believed that the book
contains a possibility of reuniting in Jesus, the man, those who
have been separated in Jesus, the Christ."[99]

96. Ibid., p. 176.
97. Ibid., p. 181.
98. A *Rabbi's Impression of the Oberammergau Passion Play* (Philadelphia: Edward Stern, 1901), p. 19.
99. Ibid., p. 12.

What follows is the attempt at a biography of Jesus. In good Reform rabbinical fashion, it seeks "to return to the sources of prophetic Judaism," after first "casting off the ritual ballast of pedantic legalism." It was the reaction of the rabbinical precisians, Krauskopf claims, which finally led to "Jesus' premature death on a Roman cross." "This is the summary of one of the saddest lives of history, of one of the noblest sons of Israel. . . . Thus stripped of mythical accretions and ecclesiastical falsifications, it is the Jew's story of the life and deeds of Jesus, the Rabbi and patriot of Nazareth."[100]

Contrary to almost all rabbinical authors, who either ignore Paul or make him responsible for the posthumous deification of Jesus, Krauskopf depicts the Apostle to the Gentiles as the benefactor of Judaism as well as humanity: "With all Paul's faults, with all the injuries his Christology has wrought, we have more reason to be grateful to him than we have cause for censure. As Jews, we are indebted to him for spreading the ethics of Judaism among a Gentile world . . . for showing us how, by the removal of obsolete, meaningless and repellant ceremonies, rites, and observances, Judaism, pure and simple, might be made a world-conquering religion."[101]

The book ends with a pious wish, reminiscent of the theology of Ebionite Jewish Christians: "What the Christian world needs is another Jew, to complete the Trinity of Jewish Reformers, one who shall combine within himself the moral and religious purity of Jesus, and the zeal and energy of Paul. He will be the long-expected Messiah. His coming will constitute the Second Advent of the Nazarene Master. The time for his coming is drawing nigh."[102]

Rabbi Krauskopf's hope, unfortunately, remains a Utopian vision—after two world wars and the murder of six million

100. Ibid., p. 143.
101. Ibid., p. 215.
102. Ibid., pp. 215–16.

Jews. We are reminded of this by the report of an ecumenical study group which accuses the Oberammergau Passion Play of 1970 of "distorting the historical and theological context of Jesus' death." The report insists that "The most dangerous feature of the play is the way it clings to medieval clichés about Jews—e.g., their avarice, enviousness, vengefulness, bloodthirstiness, treachery, insincerity, deceptiveness, fanaticism, and so forth."[103] It is hard to keep up our ecumenical optimism when we add to this the view of Rabbi Uri Themal, the study group's Jewish clergyman. Themal felt obliged to underline the fact that the Oberammergau Jesus still condemns his people (contrary to the gospel account), and still declares that the "time of grace" for the Jews has passed and that the "old covenant" is "finished," while the choir of the congregation utters the words of an eternal curse upon the Jews.

There is one rabbinical school whose position on Jesus might be summed up by the slogan *nihil novi*, since it finds that the New Testament has nothing essentially new to say. The clearest spokesman of this group was Arthur Marmorstein (1882–1941), an Orthodox rabbi from Jamnitz in Moravia. Here is his answer to the perennial Christian question, Why don't the Jews accept our faith?: ". . . if Judaism . . . in Jesus' day had long awaited a spiritual kingdom of God with moral and religious privileges and responsibilities, why then would the representatives of Judaism not receive Jesus' message? . . . Chiefly because he proclaimed no new idea, no new teaching, no new expression of any major principle. The Sermon on the Mount or one of the parables may have had a powerful effect on a cynical schoolmaster in Athens, an imperial officer in Rome who had drained the cup of pleasure to the dregs, on a merchant prince in Asia Minor with no pity for the tears of widows and orphans, on an ambitious chief magistrate in some

103. Published by the Zentralrat der Juden in Deutschland, Jüdischer Pressedienst, Düsseldorf, 1970, no. 6, p. 10.

remote provincial settlement on the Rhine or the Danube, on a simple, ordinary peasant in Spain or Gaul—but not on a genuine Jew, for the concepts, views, and doctrines taught by Jesus had long since become part of his flesh and blood."[104]

At the other end of the spectrum, Max Dienemann, an Orthodox rabbi from Offenbach (1875–1939), thought that Jesus was rejected by the majority of his fellow believers because his way of teaching and of acting had an "un-Jewish" quality about them. "Even if all the gospel accounts of Jesus' relations with the Jews were written long after the events and with a definite bias, they nevertheless reflect the historical fact that Jesus met rejection from the Jews of his time. But why was this? . . . Psychologically, the only possible explanation is that from the beginning his speech and behavior revealed features which his audience recognized at once as essentially alien to Judaism and an unwelcome departure from it. Jesus may very well not have called himself the Son of God, in the later sense of the term. But his habit of making moral demands without even trying to structure them for practical use in everyday life, of ignoring the need to relieve present troubles because the kingdom of God was already within him, must have been immediately perceived as something which was not only . . . repugnant to Jewish ethics but also certain to end up by shaking the foundations of Jewish national life. . . . Jesus' highhanded manner of commanding in the words of the Torah, along with his consciousness of personal authority must have struck his listeners as intolerable, contrary to the Jewish idea of God and the Jewish concept of prophetic mission, and an un-Jewish religious attitude.

"Only in this way can we explain why, even if he felt he had a mission to Israel, right from the start people were unwilling to recognize Jesus' claim that he wished to make of Judaism a

104. *Talmud und Neues Testament* (Jamnitz, 1908), p. 29.

deeper and more spiritual religion. With an unfailing instinct they sensed that here was something alien and destructive to Judaism."[105]

What Dienemann and other rabbis found objectionable in Jesus was his conspicuous individuality, which seemed to belie the rabbinical virtue of modesty. Rabbinical literature is not concerned with who coined a particular saying or formulated a given insight, but with what is actually taught or asserted. Leading rabbinical writers often remained anonymous or ascribed their remarks to their own teachers out of humility. "But I say to you" is indeed a familiar expression from the Talmud, legitimately used in disputations, but as the exception rather than the rule—not as in the Sermon on the Mount where it occurs repeatedly. Modern rabbis view with a no less critical eye Jesus' lack of commitment to the political and national life of Israel, as well as his total, all-monopolizing obsession with the coming kingdom of heaven, to the detriment of the here and now and the gray, depressing, day-to-day routine. His overemphasis on the ethical, some rabbis believe, left the needs of the people untouched. None of the rabbis, however, reproach him for the two tragic errors of his life—his claim to be Messiah and his notion that the kingdom of heaven was about to begin—although some are of the opinion that both these errors of judgment in the final analysis had to lead him away from Israel and closer to the Gentile world.

The first rabbi to preach in his synagogue on "Jesus and the Jews" was Stephen S. Wise (1874–1949), one of the most distinguished leaders of the American Jewish community. At the time of that sermon he was serving as President of the American Zionist Organization and the American Jewish Congress. A descendant of a well-known dynasty of Orthodox rabbis from

105. "Judentum und Urchristentum im Spiegel der neuesten Literatur," in *Monatsschrift für Geschichte und Wissenschaft des Judentums*, No. 71 (1917), p. 412.

Hungary, Wise had turned from Conservative to Reform Judaism in the course of the years. Shortly before Christmas in 1925 he chose Joseph Klausner's newly published *Jesus of Nazareth* as the subject of his Sabbath sermon. Decades later in his memoirs he summed up his thoughts at that time: "What I said that morning I had said before and said later, again and again. It was neither novel nor startling in any sense, save to such Jews and Christians as hold every barrier to be sacred. Simply and clearly I laid down the following, as I thought, undebatable theses:

1. Jesus was man, not God;
2. Jesus was a Jew, not a Christian;
3. Jews have not repudiated Jesus, the Jew;
4. Christians have, for the most part, not adopted and followed Jesus, the Jew."[106]

In the wake of international press reports, which carried his sermon throughout the world, there were four different reactions: "Monday afternoon, the President of the Orthodox rabbis' society of the country issued a blast against me and my heresy and proceded to excommunicate me. The same day an inter-denominational Christian Ministers Association met in Philadelphia and hailed me as a brother. I know not which was more hurtful—the acceptance of me as a brother and welcoming me into the Christian fold or the violent diatribe of a fellow rabbi. The liberal rabbis of the country, for the most part, rallied to my support. . . . Nothing could have been finer and more loyal than the attitude of virtually all the Zionist leaders. . . . In the midst of the excitement, a letter came to me from Nathan Straus, the grand old man of American Jewry, uniquely beloved both for his munificent philanthropies and for his warmth of heart."[107]

106. *Challenging Years*, p. 283.
107. Ibid., p. 284.

In his letter Straus urged Rabbi Wise to withdraw his resignation as head of the United Palestine Appeal and displayed full confidence in his continued leadership. The letter went on to say, "I herewith set aside an additional sum of one hundred and fifty thousand dollars ($150,000), of which amount one hundred thousand dollars ($100,000) shall be devoted to the early erection of the Nathan Straus Welfare and Relief Center of Palestine for all its needy people. . . ."[108]

Since this gift later became the cornerstone of the famous Hadassah clinic in Jerusalem, one might say that Jesus—in virtue of Klausner's book and Rabbi Wise's sermon—contributed to the healing of his fellow Jews in his old homeland.

While Stephen Wise primarily saw in Jesus the rabbinical teacher and biblical moralist, the Zionist statesman and American rabbi Abba Hillel Silver (1893–1963) felt that only the climate of messianic zeal which pervaded the land of Israel in the first century could explain the many-layered personality of Jesus: "Jesus' essential mission was apocalyptic, not prophetic. He was more of the mystic than the moralist. His impassioned concern was not to reconstruct society but to save it from the winnowing and retributive judgment which was imminent in the van of the approaching Millennium. He sought to save men from the birth-throes of the Messianic times. The ethical counsel which he gave to his followers was for a world in extremis. . . . The whole epic of Jesus must be read in the light of this millenarian chronology of his day, or it remains unintelligible. . . . He was not a revolutionist. He did not attempt to deliver his people from the yoke of Rome. He counseled no political action. It was no longer necessary. The Millennium was near and Rome would be crushed by a power greater than that of man."[109]

108. Ibid., p. 285.
109. A History of Messianic Speculation in Israel (New York: Macmillan, 1927), pp. 7–10.

In a short story entitled "The Jew and Jesus"[110] Rabbi Silver described the conversation which might have taken place "if a Jew had met Jesus on this Christmas Eve, 1936": "And the Jew would ask, 'Now that nineteen centuries have rolled by and your followers have grown from a humble little company into tens and hundreds of millions, and have mastered the Western world, where is this peace on earth? Where is the good will among men? . . . Brother Jesus, are you on your way, perhaps, this Christmas Eve, to Madrid . . . ? There you will find no heavenly hosts chanting the hymns of peace. From the skies flaming death rains down, bombs to kill men, women, and children. You will see an old Christian city with magnificent churches turned to shambles, where brother Christian is slaying brother Christian, and here they will invoke your name even as they drive bayonets into each other's bodies. Some say they kill to save your religion. Is that your religion, Brother? . . .

" 'You used to love to preach, Brother Jesus, in the synagogues. You were welcomed. Christian Germany will not let you preach in church or synagogue, for you are a Jew. They do not like Jews, even when they turn Christian. . . . They have rejected you, Brother Jesus, in the Christian world. . . . Where are you going then, on this Christmas Eve, Brother Joshua?'

"And Jesus' answer would be: 'I am not going to the magnificent cathedrals to listen to the pealing of the organ, to see the splendid robes of priestly functionaries. I am not going to smell incense. I am going through the byways of the world, even as once I walked along the shores of the Sea of Galilee seeking a few simple folk, fine honest men to help me build a Kingdom.'

" 'So am I,' the Jew would say. 'I, too, am seeking such brothers. *Shalom aleichem*—Peace be unto you!'

110. In *Therefore Choose Life: Selected Sermons, Addresses, and Writings of Abba Hillel Silver* (Cleveland: World, 1967), pp. 315–20.

" 'And unto you, Brother!' "[111]

Jewish research on Jesus is a child of Jewish polemical writing about Jesus and nineteenth-century Protestant biblical
scholarship. It inherited from its parents both its apologetic un-
dertone and its scientific curiosity. This wide-ranging scholarly
effort can be divided into three stages, all of which arose in opposition to the churches' notion of Christ. "Jesus was a Jew"
was the first, which appealed for solidarity with this lost son of
Israel. "Jesus was thoroughly Jewish" was the second phase,
which rebelled against the timeless, supernatural figure of light
created by Christology. It aimed at restoring the Nazarene to
his Jewish homeland and the rabbinical context of his life.
"Jesus was nothing but Jewish" could be the motto of the third
stage, since it set out to prove—with a certain intensity, if not
vehemence—that his teaching was not Christian and his concerns not broadly humanitarian, that his activity was meant for
Israel and not the world, and least of all the Church.

The reaction of Christian scholars to this sudden, unhoped-
for interest on the part of Jews in their unique fellow countryman also went through three stages. After the disappointment of hopes that this great thirst for knowledge might
finally lead to baptism, came a subliminal revolt against these
"pushy" attempts to de-Christianize Jesus, to reduce the Savior
of the world to a mere Jew. This discomfort led to a Pauline
shift of emphasis, away from the earthly Jesus to the post-
Easter Christ. It also led to the discovery by noted Catholic
and Protestant theologians of a series of mostly artificial an-
titheses between Jesus and Judaism. Only in the last few years
has true collaboration begun. This becomes possible when Jewish scholarship loses its polemical bite, while Christian faith
gets the courage to expose itself to the challenge of scientific
biblical criticism. Only now do we have a reasonable prospect

111. Ibid., pp. 316–20.

of discovering together that historical Jew named Yeshua, without whom the present-day civilization of the West would be unthinkable.

Gösta Lindeskog[112] has documented the breadth and diversity of Jewish interest in Jesus up until just before the outbreak of World War II. In his thirty-five-page bibliography he cites over 150 books in German from the first period of almost a century, from 1822 to 1918, but 122 titles for the twenty years from 1918 to 1938. Thanks to the greater receptivity of the English-speaking world to Judaism, the number of scholarly contributions in English to Jewish literature on Jesus has been still greater.

A considerable number of rabbis have helped to explore this virgin territory which lies between knowledge and belief. We may mention the work of two of them, men who stood at the head of the rabbinate in Hitler's Germany and Mussolini's Italy during those calamitous years just before the war.

Leo Baeck (1873–1956), the son and grandson of rabbis, was the last great municipal rabbi of Berlin and president of the Rabbinical Association in Germany until the downfall of German Judaism. As the last brilliant exponent of a thousand-year-old symbiosis, he incarnated better than anyone, perhaps, all the spiritual wealth of an unforgotten past, which had no future and which came to an end with him.

Baeck represented that German Judaism which grew up out of the fruitful dialectic between Judaism and intellectual culture. Early in his career he learned to combine the traditional doctrines of his faith with comparative religion, ethics, and philosophy. In *The Essence of Judaism* (1905) he opposed the idea of Jewish tradition to Adolf von Harnack's work *The Essence of Christianity* (1901), which the Protestant theologian had characterized as a "turning away from the anti-intellec-

112. *Die Jesusfrage im neuzeitlichen Judentum.*

tualism of the Pharisees." This tradition, Baeck wrote, "transmits the biblical heritage without a break down through the generations of those who are called to teach it. This victory over time—rather than any one great individual or any limited classical period—represents the essence of Judaism."

Even in this early work Jesus is already integrated into his overview of Judaism, just as Baeck had written in his dissertation on Spinoza, "We are proud to count Spinoza as one of us." In analyzing the opposition between Christian universalism and what Harnack calls the "narrow-minded particularism" of Judaism, he calls on Jesus as his chief witness. "I was sent only to the lost sheep of the house of Israel" (Mt 15:24). Then he deftly turns the tables on Harnack's thesis. "If the prophets addressed their message primarily and often exclusively to Israel, this was in any case a wise limitation. They knew and felt that religion first had to be firmly rooted there before it could be proclaimed to the world. Goodness had to be realized there first, true humanity had to be expressed in terms of Jewish life. . . . When Jesus wants to announce his message only to Israel and shows his disciples only this way, it testifies to the power of his preaching, not to any narrowness of his horizon. But it is just as well that these words from Matthew do not appear in the Old Testament, much less the Talmud. For otherwise they would have found little favor with the severe evangelical gentlemen engaged in Old and New Testament research. They would have been filed among the rest of the evidence for narrow-minded Jewish folk religion. The prophets speak *of* the world and its salvation, but they speak *to* Israel. Only their colorless epigones are forever summoning all of humanity to 'listen and wonder.' "[113]

Baeck then refutes with masterly brevity some of the Christian clichés about Jews, and at the same time discusses the mes-

113. *Das Wesen des Judentums,* 6th ed., p. 72.

sianic idea in Judaism in order to explain the impossibility of
Jesus' being accepted as the Jewish Messiah. "Judaism has recognized the messianic mission of Christianity and Islam. And
this realization was not dulled by the fact that Jews seldom experienced messianic treatment, especially from Christianity.
They understood the role these religions have to play in world
history, in order to make ready the course of time, and they did
not hesitate to express this openly. . . .

"Judaism cannot think of humanity without itself nor of itself without humanity. Jewish social consciousness, with its sure
sense of duty and responsibility, expands into the realm of the
broadly human, of the messianic. . . . Even before Christianity
Judaism may legitimately stress the peculiar nature of its idea
of the Messiah: It clearly acknowledges that the kingdom of
God is not something finished but in the process of development, not the religious property of the elect but the moral task
of all men. In this kingdom man sanctifies the world by blessing
God in it, by overcoming evil and doing good. The kingdom of
God lies before him, so that he may begin—before him, because it lies before all of us. All humanity is chosen. God has
sealed his covenant with humanity and hence with every individual. Human faith is believing in God and therefore in humanity, but not believing in a given belief."[114]

In barely four pages of his compilation *The Teachings of Judaism* Baeck succeeds in defining the conflict between the original Church and Pauline theology, between what Jesus believed
and belief in Jesus.[115] "The oldest Christian community—i.e.,
all those who were united in their belief that the Messiah had
appeared in the person of Jesus—lived both personally and com-
munally within the sphere of Judaism. They belong in this Jewish domain as entirely as other contemporary groups, such as, at
one end of the spectrum, the Essenes and, at the other, the

114. Ibid., pp. 275, 282.
115. *Die Lehren des Judentums* (Leipzig, 1930), pp. 56–60.

Sadducees. The thoughts and hopes cherished by the first Christians are thoroughly Jewish. They are interested only in Jewish life, their world is bounded by a Jewish horizon."

Then there was Pauline Christology, whose concept of Jesus was no longer compatible with the fundamental tenets of Judaism. "Here in Pauline theology, under the determining influence of oriental and Hellenic mystery religions, something totally different had developed out of the Jewish messianic faith of the old Christian community: the myth of Christ. Here too Jesus is the center of things. But the Jesus who is now the object of the thoughts and hopes of the faithful is no longer the same man who had warned and taught and made promises, and of whom his companions and disciples had given an account. He is now quite different, only his name is left.

"He is now the mythical Redeemer of the world, who was from the very beginning, the universal principle 'through whom all things have been made.' Faith in him becomes decisive, and God, who had been everything for Jesus, now is thrown into his shadow. The meaning of God is simply that He sent this savior into the world, that He is 'the God and Father of our Lord Jesus Christ' (Rom 15:6)."[116]

Practically all of Baeck's later ecumenical writings, such as The Pharisees, Trends in Judaism, Judaism in the Church, and The Son of Man were considered important enough by the Gestapo to be publicly burned. In the year of the Third Reich's Kristallnacht, when it became only too clear to Jews that Jesus had been lost to Christianity, Leo Baeck found the time and leisure to entertain the Jewish Jesus, his rejected brother. In the infrequent pauses from his exhausting work in the Government Agency for German Jews, where he had to beg every day for relief for the doomed, for a postponement of the inevitable brutality, he managed to complete The Gospel as a Document of

116. Ibid., pp. 56, 58.

Jewish Religious History.[117] His main concern here—light-years away from the agonies of soul he went through each day—was to restore the original gospel, to press through to the real Jesus by means of the earliest Jewish tradition. Layer by layer Baeck removes the accumulated deposits of later periods, for "only when we understand the mode of oral tradition as it flourished then in Palestinian Judaism, with its poetic sensibility and narrative techniques, can we grasp the continuities and discontinuities in the gospel story."[118]

In later layers, especially the Pauline and the Johannine, he sees Jesus elevated to "Son of God," Savior of the world, and mediator for humanity. History has thus turned into myth.[119] Beneath all this, however, the oldest accounts of Jesus speak of him "first of all" as a teacher, his disciples' "rabbi"; here is the "old message," the "first gospel tradition—in no way different from the rest of tradition in the Jewish world of those days."[120]

Baeck is well aware of the difficulties created by such a discrimination between sources in the crowded palimpsest of the gospel texts, but he believes that "on the whole it is possible to penetrate to the original text."[121] And he wants to restore this protogospel to international Judaism, which as he sees it is "catholic" enough to find room for Spinoza as well as Philo, for Josephus as well as Jesus.

On a single point Baeck finds himself in agreement with Hitler—although their premises are completely reversed. "Well, whether it's the Old Testament or the New—it's still the same Jewish bunk," said Hitler to Hermann Rauschning in 1934. Four years later, when Hitler began to draw murderous conclusions from his "understanding of the Bible," Leo Baeck wrote,

117. *Das Evangelium als Urkunde der jüdischen Glaubensgeschichte* (Berlin, 1938).
118. Ibid., p. 5.
119. Ibid., pp. 56, 60, 63.
120. Ibid., p. 67.
121. Ibid., p. 67.

"When that old tradition appears to us in this light, then the gospel, the Jewish gospel, for that is what it originally was, becomes a part, and not a negligible one, of Jewish literature. It does so, not because or not only because we find lines in it which are identical or similar to those in other Jewish documents from that time. Still less because the Hebrew or Aramaic keeps bursting out of the Greek translation, in word choice and sentence structure. The gospel is a Jewish book rather because, purely and simply because, the clear air which blows through it and which it breathes is the air of Holy Scripture. Because the Jewish spirit, and none other, holds sway in it. Because Jewish faith and Jewish hope, Jewish pain and Jewish anguish, Jewish knowledge and Jewish longing, nothing else, ring through it, one Jewish book amidst other Jewish books. Judaism may not pass it by, misjudge it, nor wish to dispense with it. In the case of the gospel Judaism should grasp what is its own and come to know it."[122]

But Baeck is less concerned with literature than with the figure of the Nazarene, the inaugurator of a whole series of "redeemers" in Israel. Writing in another book about this great line of "eschatological heralds," which stretches from Jesus to Sabbatai Zevi and includes no fewer than nineteen would-be Messiahs, he remarks, "They had a tremendous yearning to get to the end of the road," to be king, "even before the kingdom was there."[123]

Shortly before the outbreak of World War II, in a world full of hate, Leo Baeck found words that transcend the bounds of scholarship to demonstrate his true understanding and love for Jesus' teaching and his people. It sounds like one rabbi speaking across the thousands of years about another rabbi, both of them inspired with the same love for Israel and threatened by the might of the Gentiles: "In the old gospel . . . a man with

122. Ibid., p. 70.
123. *Dieses Volk, Jüdische Existenz* (Frankfurt, 1957), p. 198.

noble features stands before us. He lived in the land of the
Jews during agitated, tension-filled days, worked and helped,
suffered and died, a man from the Jewish people, who lived by
Jewish ways, in Jewish faith and hope. His spirit dwelt in the
Holy Scriptures; he thought and created in them. He announced the word of God and taught it, because God had
given him the gift of hearing and preaching the word. Before
us stands a man who won disciples from among his people.
They were looking for the Messiah, the son of David, the
promised one, and they found him in Jesus and held fast to
him. They believed in him so strongly that he began to believe
in himself and entered upon his fateful mission, and upon the
stage of world history. He haunted his disciples, and they
believed in him even after his death, so that it became the
great certainty of their existence that he had, as the prophet
foretold, 'arisen from the dead on the third day.' In this old tradition we see a man before us who shows the Jewish stamp in
all the lines and marks of his being, who reveals in them with
particular clarity all that is pure and good in Judaism. A man
who, being what he was, could only have sprung up from the
soil of Judaism—only from this land could he have gotten such
disciples and followers. A man who only here, in this Jewish domain, in Jewish confidence and longing, could go through life
and into death—a Jew among Jews. Jewish history and Jewish
thought may not pass him by nor overlook him. Since he lived,
no age has been without him, and in ages to come he will be
the point of departure."[124]

Three times Leo Baeck was given the opportunity to save
himself and his family by emigrating. Three times he turned
down the offer, which seemed to him a dereliction of duty. He
wanted to stay with his people as their rabbi and teacher "as
long as a single Jew still remained in Germany," as he wrote at

124. *Das Evangelium*, p. 69.

the time to some American friends. "'. . . as you did it to one
of the least of these my brethren, you did it to me'" (Mt 25:
40). In 1943 he arrived as a prisoner at the Theresienstadt con-
centration camp, where remained the spiritual center till the
end, "a lighthouse in a sea of tears, amid the waves of despair,"
as the history of the camp later put it. In little camp rooms, in
the wooden barracks, and beneath the open sky he gave lectures
on Plato and Kant, on Isaiah and Job—a single year-long Sermon on the Mount from the depths of abandonment, bearing
intrepid and imperturbable witness to the glad tidings of both
Testaments. "Our Father in heaven is not dead—even if men
made in His image have become inhuman monsters!"

When the Russians liberated Theresienstadt, Rabbi Baeck
by chance—or providence—belonged to the 9,000 prisoners
(out of 140,000) who survived the ordeals of the camp. "'Father, forgive them; for they know not what they do,'" Rabbi
Yeshua prayed on the Roman cross for his tormentors (Lk
23:34). In 1945 Rabbi Baeck used all his personal influence to
protect the German camp guards from acts of vengeance. And
as soon as he had recovered mentally and physically, he was
among the first to speak up for reconciliation between Germans
and Jews.

*   *   *

In 1938, shortly before the publication of Baeck's *The Gospel
as a Document of Jewish Religious History*, there appeared in
Udine a work 370 pages long entitled simply *The Nazarene*. It
was published by a Catholic press[125] just at the point when
Mussolini, under pressure from Hitler, was beginning a fragmentary imitation of his race laws—and a number of Italian Jews had
themselves baptized to escape persecution. The author of the
book was Italo Zolli, alias Israel Zoller, born in 1881 in what
was then Austrian Galicia. In Trieste he first Italianized his

125. Institute for Academic Publishing.

name to Ignazio, then Italo, and finally Italo Zolli. In 1932 he
adopted the middle name Anton in honor of St. Anthony,
whose seven-hundredth birthday was being celebrated then—
the fourth but not the last change of names for the rabbi. He
also lectured for some years at the University of Padua, a post
which at the time required membership in the Fascist party.

The Nazarene begins with a quotation from the Gospel According to John, "No one ever spoke as this man has." Then in
the first chapter Zolli shows that the appellation "Nazarene"
(Mt 2:23) derives from the Aramaic root meaning "to preach,"
for "Jesus, the great speaker and preacher, followed the customs of his time by preaching and praying in public." In the
second chapter we read that "the predictions, the prophecy of
his betrayal by Judas, of his trial, the passion, his death, and his
resurrection, as well as the persecutions his Apostles would have
to suffer—all this proves the divine quality of Jesus' foresight."

With reference to Jesus' conversation with his disciples after
the Last Supper, Zolli writes, "Jesus was never greater than at
the time he spoke the painful word: It is enough. . . . In the
passion of Jesus Christ human life is divinized. . . . The way
of Jesus leads from heaven to earth. His stay on earth was only
passing. . . . His mission was to herald the dawn of a new kingdom. Jesus represents the turning of heaven towards the earth.
Jeremiah is simply an attempt at ascending into heaven, a de-
spairing outcry of the earth to heaven. Jeremiah wants to rescue, Jesus wishes to redeem. . . ."

The next three chapters discuss Jesus' role as mediator and
his message of salvation in the sense of a liberal, but more or
less Catholic soteriology. The fact that this book, one of Zolli's
more than two dozen writings aimed at bridging the gap between Judaism and the Church, did not prevent his election as
chief rabbi (*rabbino capo*) of Rome can only be explained by
the unique and pervasive influence of Catholicism in the homeland of the Roman state church.

"Jesus enthusiasts," as they are called by Italian Jews, are therefore no oddity—but a Christian chief rabbi certainly was. For on February 13, 1945, Italo Zolli was publicly baptized in Rome, taking the name, Eugenio, of his honorary godfather, Pope Pius XII. "The figure of Christ has attracted me for years," he said shortly afterwards, and added, "This is something that I have been thinking about for years, for decades."

To this day many Jews in Rome consider Zolli a traitor or apostate. They cannot understand how he managed to function as the religious head of the Italian Jewish community, to advise them and support them in their Jewishness during those fateful years—when he was all the while coming closer to an unequivocal acceptance of Christianity. In all fairness it must be remarked that he reaped no worldly advantage from his conversion, and at the time of the great raid on the Jews in October 1943 he contributed, with help from the Pope, to the rescue of at least 850 Jews. He was by that time already speaking of Pius XII as the "Holy Father." This has led various eyewitnesses of those years of terror to Rabbi Barry Dov Schwartz's conjecture: "Many [Italian] Jews were persuaded to convert after the war, as a sign of their gratitude to that institution which had saved their lives. We may presume that such was the case with Rabbi Israel Zolli, the Chief Rabbi of Rome. . . ."[126]

Whether by coincidence or divine dispensation, the slow ripening of religious conviction at the same time and in the same country led in another instance to exactly the opposite result: Shortly after Zolli's conversion a peasant community in the Apulian village of San Nicandro underwent circumcision, embraced Judaism, and later emigrated to Israel, where they founded a village in Galilee.[127] Naturally there was no lack of

126. "The Vatican and the Holocaust," in *Conservative Judaism*, Summer, 1964, p. 46.

sensational articles in the Italian press, trying to draw up a "theological balance sheet" to determine whether the Church of Rome had gained or lost more by the two conversions.

*   *   *

The Second World War was a watershed in Jewish history. Its impact can only be compared with the second destruction of the Temple. It also led to new beginnings in the changing relations between Jews and Christians. "That cross makes me shudder. It is like an evil presence."[128] So spoke a Jewish friend to Father Edward Flannery, the first Catholic author of a comprehensive history of anti-Semitism. No wonder. From Hitler's swastika to the Hungarian arrow cross and the Rumanian St. Michael's cross, there were no fewer than eleven "Christian" parties in Europe in the years between the wars (1920–41) whose common interests extended to two things, the symbol of the cross and hatred of Jews.

On the other hand, any doubts as to the common root of both these religions of the Bible would be dispelled by a scene from the Wilna ghetto: "There was a Jew there," reports Pastor Rudolf Pfisterer, "whom the guards mockingly called 'Jew Jesus.' One day they seized him, led him out in front of the camp, wrapped a crown of barbed wire around his head, and crucified him at the entrance to the camp, to taunt both Jews and Christians together."[129]

Thus one and the same way of the cross leads from Golgotha to the gas chambers of Auschwitz. Jewish agony on the Gentile cross, Jewish faith and Gentile mockery! The greater the gap

127. I have described the religious odyssey of these simple backwoodsmen, who found their way to Judaism—and to Israel—thanks to a "village prophet," in spite of Fascism, the Gestapo, and hostility from the world around them in *The Prophet of San Nicandro* (Berlin, 1963).

128. *The Anguish of the Jews* (New York: Macmillan, 1965), p. xi.

129. *Juden, Christen—getrennt, versöhnt* (Gladbeck: Schriftenmissionsverlag, 1968), p. 50.

separating the Nazarene from Gentile Christians, the nearer
the paganization of the baptized seems to bring him back to
his own people. Isn't this rabbi bleeding on the cross the incarnation of all Israel, which, tortured and mocked like him, is
continually being crucified by the hatred for Jews? The first one
to give artistic expression to this insight was the Jewish painter
Marc Chagall, who in his "Crucifixion in Yellow" showed Jesus
as a rabbi, with his phylacteries and prayer shawl, a Jew standing before God. But for those with eyes to see, the figure suffering on this crude wooden crucifix is not a Jew but "the Jew,"
whose pain embraces all his six million murdered brothers and
sisters. To point up this message still more clearly, in Chagall's
"White Crucifixion" a crowd of concentration-camp prisoners,
pogrom victims, and Jewish refugees look up to the cross,
where the rabbi praying there seems to cry out, "Eli, Eli lama
Asavtani?" The zeal of the Galilean, his love for Israel, but
above all his tragic death have brought Jesus home to many
Jewish thinkers of the Auschwitz generation. Since the war a
number of rabbis have portrayed Jesus as a Torah preacher
whose thirst for redemption transformed him into a political
Messiah figure. Rabbi Ben Zion Bokser (born 1907), a leader of
Conservative Judaism in the United States, seeks to understand
him in this way. "The Jesus of history was a son of his people,
who shared their dreams, who was loyal to their way of life,
who died a martyr's death because of a commitment to his vision of their highest destiny."[130]

Rabbi George G. Fox, an American Reform rabbi, reminds
his Christian friends that Jews are not only Jesus' brothers "according to the flesh" but are closely tied to him "in faith and
hope." For the main concern of the Nazarene was to "make a
better world through the coming of the Kingdom." "His followers," Fox continues, "in this respect have not, to a very

130. *Judaism and the Christian Predicament* (New York: Knopf, 1967),
p. 207.

large extent, been his real disciples. But for this the Man of Nazareth is not to blame. Singularly, the real disciples of Jesus have been his own flesh and blood who have borne the whips and lashes of torture and persecution, and yet, like their great kinsman, have not given up faith either in God or the Kingdom."[131]

Some rabbis question the uniqueness of Jesus, especially in his passion and death. These, they say, are clearly the acts of a martyr, but just as clearly the bitter lot of many other Jews. Thus Rabbi R. Brasch (born 1912), a Reform rabbi from Sydney, Australia, cites Josephus concerning the "3600 Jews . . . whom the Romans, in their cruelty, scourged and crucified in a single day." He goes on to observe that "after Rome had conquered the Holy Land, an inhuman reign of terror weighed down on the Jewish people. Crucifixion in those days served the purpose of a modern firing squad, and it became an everyday event. . . . Jewish citizens who had dared to fight for their freedom were executed in this brutal fashion. Their crucified bodies, hanging from wooden crosses on the outskirts of Jerusalem, were an all too frequent sight. One of these crucified Jews was Jesus. He was one of the many thousand who had to pay for their yearning for freedom with their lives. . . . In their lust for power the Romans stifled every protest against their regime in Judea, and they saw in Jesus just another political rebel."[132]

Rabbi David De Sola Pool (1885–1970), the scion of a famous dynasty of Orthodox rabbis from Portugal, who functioned until just before his death at the oldest synagogue in New York (Shearith Israel), had no difficulty attesting to Jesus' near-orthodoxy: "As a Jew Jesus lived a fully Jewish life and observed the ritual prescriptions of the Torah. . . . He grew up

131. *The Jews, Jesus and Christ* (Chicago: Argus, 1953), p. 28.
132. *The Eternal Flame* (London, 1958), p. 64.

among the Pharisees. . . . In the tradition of the Bible he
denounced the insincere hypocrites among the Pharisees, but,
speaking of the genuinely pious ones, he said: 'The scribes and
the Pharisees sit on Moses' seat; so practice and observe whatever they tell you' [Mt 23:2–3]. . . . The religion which Jesus
preached and practiced was almost without exception Pharisaic
Judaism. The classical Pharisaic understanding of the Scrip-
ures and moral teaching had a profound influence on the Sermon on the Mount."[133]

"If I should be forced to separate my Germanness from my
Jewishness, I would not survive the operation." This remark of
Franz Rosenzweig, the great homecomer to Judaism, held a bitter truth for the Reform rabbi R. R. Geis (1906–72). At the
first opportunity he left Israel and went to Germany to fling an
unmistakable cry, hewn from the ancient rock of Jewish feeling, into the faces of Christians and Germans. His message
came from the depths of his heart—that Jewish martyrdom
made sense, all logic and history notwithstanding, that religious
dialogue with the Church after Auschwitz was not only possible but necessary, and that the former "Church triumphant,"
in its new state of powerlessness, needed "God's minority" as
never before.

Rabbi Geis's theology drew its defiance and its inextinguisha-
ble hope from the Bible of Israel. As an ecumenist, he was no
less pleased with the growing thirst for knowledge in Christian
circles about the "Jewish roots" of the Church than with the
increasing Jewish interest in Jesus. "It is significant that Judaism—scarcely set free from its fear of the churches—can
affirm Jesus the Jew in so many ways. It rediscovers in him Jewish faith, Jewish hope, Jewish knowledge, and Jewish longing,
and it does this in the face of extreme aloofness, if not active
hostility, towards Judaism on the part of Christian theology."[134]

133. Ibid., pp. 177 ff.
134. *Gottes Minorität* (Munich, 1971), p. 192.

In discussing the faith of pious Christians, Geis follows good rabbinical tradition in viewing self-sacrifice, body and soul, as the ultimate test of true religion. "It would seem to us irreverent if we as Jews overlooked the powerful faith in Jesus Christ which not long ago led many people to take upon themselves a martyr's death. And, likewise, it remains incomprehensible to us that a centuries-old martyrdom . . . should not be sufficient proof of the genuineness of Jewish belief. There is no arguing over faith for which men have lived, suffered, and fought."[135]

Rabbi Geis sees Jesus himself as a great revolutionary. In proclaiming that the time of salvation is near, "Jesus is no fantast, no moral taskmaster who overlooks or relentlessly scorns human weakness. . . . This is an unprecedented revolutionary stance; Jesus calls the entire order of human affairs into question. This speech calls for the transformation of the earth. 'Blessed are you poor, for yours is the kingdom of God. Blessed are you that hunger now, for you shall be satisfied. . . . But woe to you that are rich, for you have received your consolation' [Lk 6:20–21, 24]. Eschatological impatience pulsates in Jesus' words. One hears straightaway the vehement 'Forward, forward, forward!' Along with many Jews, most of the Christian hierarchy want to have nothing to do with this revolutionary Jesus. But that in no way alters or weakens his message. The man of mercy, the champion of justice, and peacemaker comes to the fore. The principalities and powers of this world fade away. Indeed, the demands he makes of man in view of the coming kingdom of God can become so madly excessive that the believer already begins to live in that kingdom—in a world which is not yet ready for it. The Sermon on the Mount is a single tremendous leap of anticipation. In this connection we must not forget, not even for a moment, that Jesus is a Jew and speaks only the language of his people. *Malchuth Sha-*

135. Ibid.

mayim, literally translated as the kingdom of heaven, means nothing more or less than the kingdom of God on earth. The only reason for the word "heaven" is that as a Jew Jesus shrinks from mentioning the name of God. As a Jew Jesus means by 'redemption' a public act on the stage of history. Only in virtue of this is there any redemption for the individual soul. The man who asks, in the Sermon on the Mount, 'Is not life more than food, and the body more than clothing?' does not let himself get shunted off into the other world—that would take the edge off his powerful, insistent words. This is the only thing that concerns us with Jesus' sermon. It does not 'interest' us; it grabs hold of us. A man arises to take up where the prophets left off, to thrust their teaching forward to the dawn of salvation, to burn into the souls of all of us, whether Christians or Jews, an image of man that ought to leave us perpetually dissatisfied with man as he is. Christians and Jews may shake their heads. . . ."

Rabbi Geis's teachers, Leo Baeck, Martin Buber, and David Flusser, all stress in different ways Jesus' place in the religious history of Israel. He quotes them approvingly, and then comes to this optimistic conclusion: ". . . in the Christian world a new frame of mind is making its appearance. Unless I am very much mistaken, Jesus' message of salvation for the kingdom of God on earth can once more be heard in its concrete directness. The long-cherished, almost exclusive involvement with the 'religious ego' pales before the kingdom of God. . . ."[136]

A Jewish Understanding of the New Testament[137] offers what is almost certainly the first purely scientific study undertaken by a rabbi of the Christian Scriptures. Its author, Reform Rabbi Samuel Sandmel (born 1914), is provost and professor of Bible and Hellenistic literature at Hebrew Union College in

136. Ibid., p. 227.
137. New York: University Publishers, 1960.

Cincinnati, where he is justly famous for his elucidation of difficult theological questions. "The New Testament," he writes in his first chapter, "is a religious book, the product of a religious community which believed that it had received a heritage of God's revelation. In this sense, it is not history, though history is in it; nor a story book, though stories are in it. Rather, it is a testimony to the assumption that all things are possible to God, and therefore it is also a record of those things which it believed happened."[138]

Throughout the book Rabbi Sandmel sheds light on the gospel from a Jewish point of view: "The true genius of the New Testament is that, like the rabbinic halaka, it sets forth an interpretation of the will of God. Like the Old Testament and rabbinic law, it envisages an Israel, a body of believers, a Church. The distinctiveness of the New Testament is its commitment to 'faith' as it is mediated by the Church, which collected and preserved the writings and canonized them. The exaltation of faith is both the strength of the New Testament, and also its exposure to weakness."[139]

He can summarize the "bare facts" on Jesus in a few lapidary lines: "Jesus, who emerged into public notice in Galilee when Herod Antipas was its Tetrarch, was a real person, the leader of a movement. He had followers, called disciples. The claim was made, either by him or for him, that he was the long-awaited Jewish Messiah. He journeyed from Galilee to Jerusalem, possibly in 29 or 30, and there he was executed, crucified by the Romans as a political rebel. After his death, his disciples believed that he was resurrected, and had gone to heaven, but would return to earth at the appointed time for the divine judgment of mankind."[140]

No less objective and free of apologetic intent is Reform

138. Ibid., p. 9.
139. Ibid., p. 314.
140. Ibid., p. 33.

Rabbi Morris Goldstein (born 1904) from San Francisco, whose collection *Jesus in the Jewish Tradition*[141] was his doctoral dissertation at Hebrew Union College. The purpose of his work is to find answers to two key questions which are both inseparable and contradictory and which have always placed a terrible burden on theology: Why was Jesus born in the nation of Israel? And why did Israel reject his teaching?

To the more personal question of why a rabbi would devote almost eight years of his life to research into the life of Jesus, Rabbi Goldstein has four answers: "To acquire a clearer understanding of Judaism . . . to open up historical source material to students of Christianity . . . to promote Christian-Jewish dialogue and . . . to produce a continuous historic account of the Jewish viewpoint on Jesus."[142] However, since Rabbi Goldstein's textual analysis goes only as far as the end of the eighteenth century, which he rightfully calls "the end of the Jewish Middle Ages," the results of his research have today only a fragmentary value and have been partially superseded by later studies.

Less cautious but of more immediate interest is the work of Rabbi Goldstein's brother, Rabbi Israel Goldstein, one of the leading figures of Conservative Judaism in America and a cofounder of the National Conference of Christians and Jews. In a 1972 sermon addressed to his Bnai-Jeshurun congregation in New York and entitled "A Jewish View of Jesus," he meditates on what Jesus' brothers might think of him if Christians had taken the idea of imitating him seriously. "It is a subject worth pondering—how would Jews today feel about Jesus, if Jewish communities had not been crucified over and over again in his name, in every age of so-called Christian civilization. I assume Jews would think he was a charismatic teacher, who wished to emphasize the spirit, not the letter, of the Torah; a man who

141. New York: Macmillan, 1950.
142. Ibid., pp. 3, 5, 9–14.

rebelled against the Establishment of his day; who mixed with the poor and the oppressed . . . and . . . who was quite understandably repudiated by the religious authorities as a threat to the survival of the Jewish way of life, since they considered adherence to the law the best guarantee of their national existence. In Christian consciousness Jesus is the product of centuries of mythologization. In Jewish consciousness he is what the Church has made of him, and the persecutions which have been carried out in his name."[143]

At the opening of the biennial conference of American Reform rabbis which took place in Chicago in November 1963, its president, Rabbi Morris N. Eisendrath, made a ringing appeal for a new evaluation of Jesus' role as a rabbi—"the man Jesus, not Christ!" as he made emphatically clear. In his opening address he said this to his colleagues: "Are we to remain adamant —orthodox—in our refusal to examine our own . . . interpretations of the significance of the life of Jesus, the Jew? . . . How long can we persist in ignoring his lofty and yet so simply stated prophetic and rabbinic teachings, merely on the grounds that he repeated much that was voiced by his prophetic predecessors and rabbinic contemporaries? Was Micah more spiritually and morally original than Amos and Hosea? Do none of the rabbis we revere and whose utterances we have our children master repeat each other? . . . How long before we can admit that his influence was a beneficial one—not only to the pagans but to the Jews of his time as well, and that only those who later took his name in vain profaned his teaching? . . . I would hope that we, too, have grown up sufficiently in our religious security and as the world's most adult religion in terms of seniority, that we can now afford to render unto Jesus that which is Jesus's without blanching or self-flagellation. . . . I therefore recommend that our Commission on Interfaith Activities make

143. From the original text of the sermon, for which I thank Rabbi Goldstein.

a special study of this burning issue as a tangible contribution to that ecumenicity we ask others to effect in our behalf."[144]

The single dissonant note—for sensitive Jewish ears—in Rabbi Eisendrath's speech was sounded in words which, though spoken in Chicago before a group of rabbis, were addressed to a group of bishops in Rome, where the Second Vatican Council was struggling, amid passionately polarized opinions, over the so-called "Jewish Schema": "While much if not most of what happens under Michelangelo's magnificent dome is related to internal church structure and policy, the work of the Secretariat for Promoting Christian Unity . . . remains of particular interest to Jews. We Jews are paying special attention to this organ of the Church in hopes that its efforts may finally lead to that long awaited reassessment of the Church's relations to Jews and Judaism."[145]

Then Rabbi Eisendrath proposed something which sounds almost like a theological barter—recognition of Jesus in exchange for repudiation of Jewish "deicide": "The mind is elated, the heart is cheered by the prospect of the official revocation of that age-old accusation brought against the Jewish people by the Catholic Church. . . . Interfaith understanding, based on mutual respect, is no longer a one-way street. We Jews have long called for this indispensable change in Catholic preaching and exegesis. What now will be our attitude as Jews to Christianity, and in particular to Jesus?"[146]

James Parkes is an Anglican priest who in 1964 published the complete text of Eisendrath's address in his book *Jewry and Jesus of Nazareth*. As a Judaist and ecumenist, he takes a position which was welcomed by many rabbis in England, Canada, and the United States: "It may help to clarify the historic chal-

144. Morris Eisendrath and James Parkes, *Jewry and Jesus of Nazareth* (King's Langley, England: The Parkes Library, 1964), p. 6.
145. Ibid., p. 5.
146. Ibid., pp. 5 ff.

lenge contained in Rabbi Eisendrath's recent proposal, if I add that Christians must first rediscover the Jewish Sinai-experience before we can expect Jews to want to discover Christ. . . . In the name of Jesus Jews have suffered persecutions and injustice for two thousand years. In his name they were murdered by the thousands and tens of thousands. In his name they were forced to accept baptism and robbed of their children. Christians, on the other hand, have never suffered in the name of the Sinai nor been persecuted on account of the Torah. It is therefore only right and just that the first step towards rapprochement come from the Christians—and not simply in words."[147]

Eisendrath's suggestion and similar initiatives on the part of Reform rabbis led to a renewed burst of Christian missionary hopes, eloquently expressed by the late Jean Cardinal Daniélou, S.J. After noting with satisfaction that "some of the best books about Jesus" published in recent years "have been written by Jews," the prince of the Church wondered out loud why Jews were unwilling to take one further step and "to recognize in Jesus the fulfillment of the Law."[148]

Rabbi Jacob B. Agus (born 1911), a well-known Reform rabbi who also holds a theological chair at Temple University in Philadelphia, was asked to respond to Cardinal Daniélou, and he took this opportunity to destroy some baseless illusions: ". . . to ask Jews to recognize in Jesus 'the fulfillment of the Law' is to give an excellent demonstration of the folly of transposing the subjective content of one faith into the subjective structure of another faith. . . . In the private realm of religious feelings and symbols, comparison involves the fullest analysis of what Catholics mean by 'Jesus,' by 'fulfillment,' by 'the Law.' Then, it is necessary to plumb similarly the primary, secondary, and ineffable meanings of the term 'Torah,' to Jews.

147. Ibid., p. 8.
148. *Dialogue with Israel, with a response by Rabbi Jacob B. Agus* (Baltimore: Helicon, 1968), p. 69.

And it is needful to choose one out of many versions of the historical Jesus or one out of many versions of the Christian image
of Jesus, and then determine the content of 'fulfillment' in respect of Torah and Jesus. It would be easier to move geometric
figures into a non-Euclidean world."[149]

Spokesmen such as Rabbi Agus, who underscore the breadth
of the abyss of misunderstanding between Jews and Christians,
also show the pressing need to initiate a realistic religious dialogue. After almost two thousand years of exaggerating the
things that separate us, it is time to talk about our common
roots. That is the intent of Rabbi Roland Gradwohl (born
1931) from Bern in his report "The New Understanding of
Jesus in Contemporary Jewish Thought."[150] While he rejects
all forms of syncretism and, like Martin Buber, warns of "the
pitfall of artificial common interests," he concludes on a positive note that "Jesus is an immense figure in Jewish religious
history. . . . Regardless of our different positions we must promote Jewish-Christian dialogue now more than ever. Jesus is, as
it were, the clasp which binds Jews and Christians together in
mutual respect. He shows them the way to their common goal:
the brotherhood of all men in a world of freedom and security
—in belief in God and the meaning of life."[151]

Still rare, but unmistakable, are the voices of Orthodox rabbis
who recognize Jesus not only as a Jewish brother but also as a
fellow rabbi. For example, Rabbi Jacob Posen from Zurich
writes, "It becomes increasingly clear how deeply rooted Christianity is in Judaism, and how unintelligible Jesus' teachings
are if you remove them from their historical setting. For, far
from opposing the Pharisees, Jesus was himself a rabbi; and his

149. Ibid., pp. 119–20.
150. "Das neue Jesus-Verständnis bei jüdischen Denkern der Gegenwart,"
in *Freiburger Zeitschrift für Philosophie und Theologie*, 20 (1973), part 3,
306–23.
151. Ibid., p. 323.

ideas were in no sense incompatible with their way of thinking."[152] Rabbi Posen then quotes the Jewish religious historian Hans Joachim Schoeps: "Judaism is waiting for the coming of the Messiah, Christianity for the return of Christ. It could be that the Messiah awaited by the Synagogue and the returning Christ whom the Church looks forward to, bear the same features."

Christians and Jews may possibly be united by the Messiah, but until he comes, they remain divided. And even Jesus, newly evaluated and demythologized, is not able, not yet anyway, to bridge the gap between his brothers and his disciples. This is what Rabbi Samuel Sandmel seeks to make emphatically clear in his book *We Jews and Jesus*—however much it may distress some ecumenists: "I must say most plainly that Jesus has no bearing on me in a religious way. . . . I am aware that some Christians declare that they see in Christianity, with its figure of Jesus, a completeness which eludes them in Judaism. I am not sensible of any such incompleteness, for I neither feel nor understand that my Judaism is in any way incomplete."[153]

So it seems that the old antagonism between the "Jesus of the Jews" and the "Christ of the Christians" has been replaced by a theological truce. This is a far cry from the hostility of the Middle Ages, but it is equally far from the ecumenical amity which the Nazarene strove so passionately for. Unless, perhaps, new insights may be forthcoming from the land of the Bible, where everything began. "Ever since the new settlement began, a special interest in Jesus has been manifested. This does not indicate, as some Christian theologians have wishfully stated, a turning toward Christianity. It does, however, show that in the free atmosphere of Israel a new approach toward Jesus, re-

152. "200 Jahre christlich-jüdischer Dialog," in *Christlich-jüdisches Forum*, February 1971, p. 24.
153. *We Jews and Jesus* (New York: Oxford University Press, 1965), p. 111.

moved from the realm of polemics or vituperation common to medieval Judaism, is taking place. It is to be expected that in the land where Jesus lived and from which the Christian message went forth, a deep interest should be stirred among Jews."[154] Thus wrote Reform Rabbi David Polish (born 1910), a vice-president of the Central Conference of American Reform Rabbis, in a book which backs his assumption with an impressive series of quotations from modern Hebrew literature.

Abraham Isaac Kook (1865–1935) was the first chief rabbi of Palestine, a bulwark of orthodoxy and world famous for his decisions in matters of religious law. Among his other theological concerns, he also dealt with the problem of Christianity. In an essay entitled "The Road to Renewal," which first appeared in 1909, he outlined his position: "The force which directs the world towards the absolute good is a spiritual illumination from the Divine source of all existence. This illumination is initially experienced by certain qualified individuals who channel it to society. . . . This inflow of psychic and spiritual energy may, in fact, be distorted and become a source of idolatrous aberrations. . . . Too often, however, the study of texts and the concern with the prescribed code of religious discipline, were exaggerated. The crystallizations of past achievements became the sole expression of Jewish religious life. Vision and illumination atrophied. The peril in such atrophy was the reaction it stimulated; the rise of Christianity and of the false messiahs, Shabbetai Zevi and Jacob Frank."[155]

However that may be, Rabbi Kook insists that Jesus' spirituality was authentic. His comments on the Galilean run as follows: "Christianity, which has done so much harm to the Jewish people, arose in just such a period of weakness. Its founder was a charismatic personality who exerted enormous influence.

154. *The Eternal Dissent* (London: Abelard-Schuman, 1961), p. 207.
155. Rabbi Ben Zion Bokser, "Rav Kook: The Road to Renewal," in *Tradition: A Journal of Orthodox Thought*, Winter 1973, pp. 137–38.

But for all the intensity of spiritual power which radiated from him, he did not escape the taint of idolatry. . . . Thus he and his disciples devoted themselves exclusively to the fostering of a spiritual life. They soon lost touch with the characteristic elements of Judaism, and alienated themselves in word and deed from the sources they originally sprang from."[156]

In his further remarks Rabbi Kook underlines the fact that "the little bit of good in Jesus was never completely lost, but still survives and could lead to a renewal of the soul and to an altogether necessary protest against any form of Judaism which was too one-sidedly dependent on the study of the texts . . . and the practical observance of religious laws."[157]

As far as I can tell, there are many rabbis in Israel today who would be only too glad to discuss Christianity, to take part in ecumenical dialogues, and to promote further Christian-Jewish collaboration. Thus far no rabbinical writer in Israel has undertaken to develop Rabbi Kook's ideas and to draw new conclusions from them. Perhaps the wounds of crucifixion have not yet healed—the memory of the gas chambers is still too vivid. No new Maimonides, no second Saadia has yet appeared in Jerusalem. That calls for a longer period of peace and tranquillity than Israel has been granted to date. Perhaps the next step towards biblical ecumenism may come from America, where a well-known Reform rabbi and a Catholic theologian recently co-authored a manual for religious dialogue. The chapter "Jesus" opens with the following words: "Apart from the Hebrew Bible and other values which they revere in common with the Jews, Christians have a further bond with Judaism in the person of Jesus, his mother, all the Apostles, and most of the first Christians. Jesus Christ was a Jew. Since Christians believe that Jesus is God become man, they also believe that God

156. "The Road to Renewal" [in Hebrew], in *Nir* (Jerusalem, 1909), p. 7.
157. Ibid., pp. 8–9.

became man in a Jew. In other words, Christians worship a
Jew. And Jesus was no lukewarm, uprooted Jew. As his genealo-
gies show, he was of Jewish origin; he read the Holy Scriptures,
studied, prayed with the rabbis in the synagogue, and believed
passionately in God's promises. He undoubtedly stood in the
mainstream of the Jewish prophetic tradition. Christians believe, of course, that he was more than a prophet, but that in
no way diminishes his Judaism. Jesus himself said, 'Salvation is
from the Jews' [Jn 4:22]."[158]

158. Dr. Leonard Swidler and Rabbi Marc H. Tannenbaum, *Jewish-
Christian Dialogues* (Washington, D.C., 1966), pp. 6 ff.

U